DEVELOP INTERCULTURAL COMPETENCE

HOW TO LEAD CROSS-RACIAL AND CROSS-CULTURAL CHURCHES

HiRho Y. Park

HIGHER EDUCATION & MINISTRY
General Board of Higher Education and Ministry
THE UNITED METHODIST CHURCH

Develop Intercultural Competence: How to Lead Cross-Racial and Cross-Cultural Churches

The General Board of Higher Education and Ministry leads and serves The United Methodist Church in the recruitment, preparation, nurture, education, and support of Christian leaders–lay and clergy–for the work of making disciples of Jesus Christ for the transformation of the world. Its vision is that a new generation of Christian leaders will commit boldly to Jesus Christ and be characterized by intellectual excellence, moral integrity, spiritual courage, and holiness of heart and life. The General Board of Higher Education and Ministry of The United Methodist Church serves as an advocate for the intellectual life of the church. The Board's mission embodies the Wesleyan tradition of commitment to the education of laypersons and ordained persons by providing access to higher education for all persons.

Develop Intercultural Competence: How to Lead Cross-Racial and Cross-Cultural Churches

ISBN 978-1-945935-33-6

All web addresses were correct and operational at the time of publication.

18 19 20 21 22 23 24 25 26 27–10 9 8 7 6 5 4 3 2 1

Manufactured in the United States of America

Contents

Introduction

The United Methodist Church (UMC) is a worldwide church with the distinctive mark of "connectionalism" as the conciliar principle. Being a worldwide church means that we United Methodists affirm our unity in Christ regarding missional and structural accountability, responsibility, and interdependence for the transformation of the world. The UMC recognizes that many colonial rules and cultures are still influential and dominant in the formerly colonized world. As a worldwide church, The UMC prefers to create a just and inclusive human community against postcolonialism. Being a worldwide church is a prophetic declaration that United Methodists resist racism, sexism, and classism within institutional ideologies. But this also means that The UMC must be aware and attuned to the richness and challenges posed by cross-racial and cross-cultural contexts.

This book explores ways leaders can be more effective in cross-racial and cross-cultural contexts through the experience of The UMC. The words *cross-racial and cross-cultural* (CR-CC) highlight racial dynamics in a multicultural environment, which many leadership theories have often ignored. Primarily, cross-racial and cross-cultural leadership has been a matter of racial-ethnic leaders trying to lead in a Caucasian-majority setting, not vice versa.

In this text, care has been taken in regard to the word *diversity*, because it has become associated with justice issues in a global context. In the United States people often ignore diversity training because they feel they are already living amid diversity, which is true. But that doesn't mean they are living in it *well*. Peter G. Northouse defines diversity as "the existence of different cultures or ethnicities within a group or an organization."[1] So, how do we coexist as different people? And what kind of skill sets do leaders need to lead effectively in an increasingly cross-racial and cross-cultural climate?

The United Methodist Church boldly claims, "We commit ourselves to crossing boundaries of language, culture, and social or economic status. We commit ourselves to be in ministry with all people, as we, in faithfulness to the gospel, seek to grow in mutual love and trust."[2] The UMC defines deployment of their clergy in a CR-CC context as follows:

> Cross-racial and cross-cultural appointments are made as a creative response to increasing racial and ethnic diversity in the church and in its leadership. Cross-racial and cross-cultural appointments are appointments of clergypersons to congregations in which the majority of their constituencies are

---

1   Peter G. Northouse and Marie Lee, *Leadership Case Studies in Education* (Thousand Oaks, CA: Sage Publications, 2016), loc. 151, Kindle.

2   The United Methodist Church, *The Book of Discipline of The United Methodist Church 2016* (Nashville: United Methodist Publishing House, 2016), ¶125, 96. Hereinafter *Book of Discipline 2016*.

different from the clergypersons' own racial/ ethnic and cultural background.[3]

CR-CC ministry is a unique feature of The UMC that sets it apart from many other Christian churches,[4] because United Methodists try to live out their faith by deliberately engaging in cross-racial and cross-cultural ministry. United Methodist clergy make a covenant to serve any church their bishop asks them to serve when they are ordained. This includes a church where the majority of its members are not from the same racial and ethnic background as the pastor. CR-CC ministry is an intentional endeavor of The United Methodist Church to live out their commitment to be an inclusive body of Christ. The UMC is determined to eradicate a path of powerful postcolonial discourse through cross-racial and cross-cultural ministry. We believe that CR-CC ministry is a calling of The UMC and one way that we can contribute to a world divided by ideological, political, and theological differences. Yet, leaders must be equipped to find the rewards

---

3 *Book of Discipline 2016*, locs. 7156–59.

4 *Book of Discipline 2016*, locs. 1032–38. "Inclusiveness of the Church—The United Methodist Church is a part of the church universal, which is one Body in Christ. The United Methodist Church acknowledges that all persons are of sacred worth. All persons without regard to race, color, national origin, status, or economic condition, shall be eligible to attend its worship services, participate in its programs, receive the sacraments, upon baptism be admitted as baptized members, and upon taking vows declaring the Christian faith, become professing members in any local church in the connection. In The United Methodist Church no conference or other organizational unit of the Church shall be structured so as to exclude any member or any constituent body of the Church because of race, color, national origin, status or economic condition."

and meet the challenges of serving in various contexts. They must be sensitive to otherness in their congregations and communities, so they can become better bridge builders among God's people.

The UMC CR-CC Ministry History

In 1982 the General Commission on Religion and Race (GCORR) of The UMC published "Eight Principles to Undergird Serious Reflection and Action on Open Itineracy" and initiated a discussion on the equal opportunity for clergy to serve a church regardless of racial and cultural background. *Open itineracy* means UMC clergy are deployed "without regard to race, ethnic origin, gender, color, disability, marital status, or age, except for the provisions of mandatory retirement."[5] The Council of Bishops established the Center for United Methodist Pastoral Exchange, which was located at Gammon Theological Seminary in Atlanta, Georgia, in 1983. Bishop L. Scott Allen, who was the first African American bishop in the Southeastern Jurisdiction, became the director. The Center for United Methodist Pastoral Exchange sponsored three national seminars to arouse the conscience of the church to actualize and concretize the concern for inclusiveness and equal deployment of UMC clergy, including a National Seminar on Open Itineracy in 1985 and the National Seminar for Annual Conference Leadership on Racial Inclusiveness and Ministerial Deployment in 1988. Unfortunately, the center closed in 1988 when Bishop Allen left office. After 1988 there was little discussion about open itinerancy in the denomination until 1997, when the General

---

5   *Book of Discipline 2016*, ¶425.1, 347.

Board of Higher Education and Ministry (GBHEM) started to work with Korean American clergy who were serving cross-racial and cross-cultural appointments.

In 1997 the Association of Korean American Clergy Serving Cross-Racial Appointments (AKACSCRA) was established, supported by GBHEM. The association was the first grassroots UM clergy networking organization supporting pastors in CR-CC appointments. AKACSCRA not only provided a safe space for peer support and mentoring of Korean American UM pastors who were serving CR-CC churches but also trained younger clergy who had potential to serve CR-CC congregations. At present, more than 450 Korean American United Methodist clergy are serving in CR-CC appointments.

In 1999 GBHEM published the first book about CR-CC appointments, *Witness from the Middle: Korean-American Pastors in Non-Korean Local Churches in The United Methodist Church.* This was the first publication describing the experiences of racial-ethnic clergy who had been serving in CR-CC ministry in the denomination.

In my research, I point to two elements that have been missing denominationally but that are crucial to a successful CR-CC ministry: (1) a definition of CR-CC appointment and (2) a pretraining both for clergy and congregations whenever CR-CC appointments are made.[6] GBHEM initiated legislation in 2008, and The UMC came up with the definition of a CR-CC appointment in *The Book of Discipline* and required a pretraining for clergy and congregations: "When such appointments are made, bishops, cabinets, and boards of

---

6   HiRho Y. Park, "Creating Christian Community Through the Cross-Racial Appointment: Problems and Challenges" (PhD diss., Wesley Theological Seminary, 2000).

ordained ministry shall provide specific training for the clergypersons so appointed and for their congregations."[7]

GBHEM published *Meeting God at the Boundaries: Cross-Cultural-Cross-Racial Clergy Appointments* in 2003 and a manual for church leaders in 2011. GBHEM and GCORR then collaborated to organize a denominational summit on being an inclusive church, the Facing the Future conference, in 2011. This event was designed to help the denomination resource leaders and encourage dialogue to help carry out effective CR-CC ministry. The UMC was seeking new ways of developing relevant leadership in response to the increasing racial, gender, and cultural diversity among clergy and local churches.

Foundations of CR-CC Ministry

The UMC practices CR-CC ministry based on these theological foundations:

- All people are created in the image of God (Gen 1:26–31; Acts 17:24–26). CR-CC ministry affirms the dignity and the absolute value of all people from the perspective of the Creator God.
- A church is an alternative human community (Acts 17:22–34). Relationality is a characteristic of creation. The relationality of creation is only valuable when there are intentional efforts to connect and honor each other. CR-CC ministry intends to establish a community of "shalom" that pursues wholeness by promoting unity and peace among diverse people.
- Christian faith upholds a gift of diversity (Gen 11:1–9; Acts 2). The scattering of languages in the story of

---

7   *Book of Discipline 2016*, ¶425.4, 348.

the Tower of Babel symbolizes God's way of warning against self-serving and self-preserving ethnocentrism. Ethnocentrism is the belief that one's cultural values and beliefs are the best and that one possesses the superior culture over another. CR-CC ministry affirms that people have different gifts, and we are called to learn from one another.

- Christians are called to the ministry of reconciliation (2 Cor 5:19–20). Here, reconciliation is the overcoming of alienation, estrangement, hostility, and enmity through the Spirit of Christ. The ultimate goal of CR-CC ministry is to help people bear with one another in love and grace, acknowledging our differences (Eph 4:1–6).

How to Use This Book

This book is designed to explore what makes for an effective leadership style in a cross-racial and cross-cultural context, and to provide practical guidelines and skills to lead with competence in such a context. Each chapter presents reflection questions so that a small group, whether from a church or from an organization, can study together. To start, case studies are presented sharing experiences of cross-racial and cross-cultural ministry. Using case studies, you will have an opportunity to reflect on real-life CR-CC situations, with cases involving immigration issues, theological differences, racism, the intersection of racism and sexism, language barriers, and culture clash. You can then discuss these difficult issues among a group of people with diverse perspectives in a nonthreatening environment.

Within the pages of this book, leadership theories are reviewed that can enhance cross-racial and cross-cultural leadership skills and help provide a framework for making practical decisions. An examination follows of how some of these leadership theories have been used by those who have engaged in cross-racial and cross-cultural ministry in The UMC. The characteristics of successful leaders in a cross-racial and cross-cultural context are identified, and what it means to be a human community where people get along in spite of their differences is explored. Reflections also appear on a theological understanding of "otherness" and how an understanding of otherness may create a people-centered faith community, with the needs of people as its priority. Finally, how to create a vital faith community in an increasingly cross-racial and cross-cultural society is explored. Preaching, worship, music, and prayer are Christian practices that can connect Christians beyond racial, ethnic, and cultural differences. How do you prepare a sermon that brings people together without losing interracial and intercultural dynamics? What kind of liturgy or music will promote the unity of diverse people during the worship service? These are the types of questions we will address in the chapters ahead.

> The goal of this book is to explore ways of leading an organization beyond mere tokenism.

A new way of leading people is called for as the world becomes more interconnected, with a convergence of cultures. We are called to be wounded leaders who build relationships, break stereotypes, continuously learn, and disrupt marginality. The goal of this book is to explore ways of leading an organization beyond mere tokenism, which can be pervasive in a multicultural society but which can be viewed as covert discrimination. It is easy to pretend that your organization is diverse when you have token individuals either as a leader or members. But this symbolic effort at diversity only generates performance pressure and vulnerability for such a leader, and subtle isolation and insincere treatment among members of a community. This book will assist all who seek to exercise genuine and respectful leadership in a cross-racial and cross-cultural context. Though it is based on Christian experiences, we hope that it will be helpful to leaders like you, who long to create a world in which global citizenship is the norm, both now and for future generations.

I would like to express special gratitude to all those who contributed to this book. Rev. Dr. Jung Sun Oh, a colleague who wrote a few case studies and chapter 4, furnished this book with his extensive experience serving Caucasian-majority congregations. His academic work and practical perspective provide a unique resource to the Christian community. I have been working with racial-ethnic lead pastors who have served large Caucasian-majority churches since 2011. They willingly shared their professional insights about their cross-racial and cross-cultural leadership experiences in this book. They are: Rev. Dr. Kevin James, pastor of Palm Coast UMC, Palm Coast, FL; Rev. Don Lee, pastor of First UMC of Denton, Denton, TX; Rev. Dr. Jon E. McCoy, pastor of Hinsdale UMC, Hinsdale, IL; Rev. William B. Meekins Jr., pastor of First UMC of McKeesport, PA; and Rev. Dr. Albert Shuler, pastor of New Creation UMC, Durham, NC. I am also grateful to the GBHEM Publishing Office staff, Rev. Dr. Kathy Armistead, Publisher, and Jennifer M. Rogers, EDP Senior Specialist, for their unfailing patience and support.

The Practice of Cross-Racial and Cross-Cultural Ministry

The Case Study Approach

A case study is a real-life story, an authentic situation taken from one person's perspective. Life is full of uncertainty, and we all try to discern what to do in the midst of the complexity of particular situations. Case studies expose possible scenarios of what could be done; and often, there is more than one acceptable solution to a case. A good case always presents a recognizable dilemma. The purpose of this chapter is to provide practical tips to church leaders and clergy who are leading cross-racial and cross-cultural churches, not to just inform them about theories. We hope that your church or institution takes advantage of these cases to address situations in your own experience.

Leading in a multicultural context with cross-racial and cross-cultural intricacies can be intriguing yet confusing. We often face a dilemma in a multicultural setting because we can't see alternative solutions. This is true for many local churches. Using a case study for cross-racial and cross-cultural ministry is intended to help readers merge their knowledge and experience into a thoughtful discussion so that they may, as a group, explore possible solutions to complex issues. The best solution begins with deep listening as participants seek to articulate their thoughts. The group has to learn to live with ambiguity, which is a critical learning point whenever we encounter a cross-racial and cross-cultural situation. A case study assumes that all participants bring skills, insights, and knowledge; therefore, different perspectives are respected and honored. Remember: there may be more than one acceptable solution for each case. As we participate in a case study, both facilitator and participants learn from each other; the discussion is based on mutual learning.

The following case studies present issues and dilemmas we often face in cross-racial and cross-cultural contexts.

- The first case study presents a controversial social issue around US immigration policies. How do Christians welcome strangers when they are undocumented immigrants?
- The second case study begs the question, how should Christians approach the issue of hate? This case study involves, among other incidents, the infamous mass shooting of African Methodist Episcopal Church members in Charleston, South Carolina, by a white supremacist.
- The third case study helps us think about the issue of poverty, which we cannot ignore when we live in a multicultural society. What is a Christian response to poverty?
- The fourth case study illustrates the intersection of racism and sexism. It describes a racial-ethnic woman pastor who is part of a clergy couple serving a Caucasian-majority church.

- The fifth case study deals with language differences. Reverend Lee, who speaks English as a second language, finds both joys and struggles serving a Caucasian-majority church.
- The last case study describes a situation of working collaboratively across race, culture, and countries as issues arise with administration.

At the end of each case, we ask three (or more) questions that will assist you in exploring the case. We also provide some resources that will enhance your learning.

How to Study a Case

Preparation: It is strongly recommended that you have a flip chart and a person acting as scribe. All participant comments should be recorded so that the group can see them and remember them for the best result.

Time needed: Approximately one and one-half hours

Step One: Choose a facilitator, specifically, someone who is excited about leading a case study. The facilitator needs to know the members of the discussion group and be trusted by them. The focal point of a case study is the participants and their insights, not the facilitator's teaching. The facilitator encourages the participants to review the case in advance and to bring resources related to the issue.

Step Two: Read the case carefully, beforehand if possible. Sometimes, reading together helps with different voices and accents.

Step Three: Analyze the characters in the story. Who are they? Where are they coming from? What do they do? Why are they doing that?

Step Four: Write down a chronological sequence of the events.

Step Five: Name the issues and share possible solutions to the problem or dilemma.

Step Six: Share resources regarding the case.

Step Seven: Each person shares what he or she has learned from the case and how he or she would respond to the issue presented. By listening carefully to others, a person may want to change his or her position. If that happens, it is okay.

Case Study 1: Immigration

Arch Street United Methodist Church in Philadelphia has been home for Javier Flores Garcia since November 13, 2016.

Flores, originally from Mexico, was due to surrender to Immigration and Customs Enforcement (ICE) but turned to the church instead. Rev. Robin Hynicka said Garcia, now in his forties, has been living peacefully in the church and volunteers for many church programs, especially those with homeless people.

"His son, Javier Jr., stays overnight most nights. He is 5 and he just does not want to leave his father's side," Hynicka said.[1]

Since the news of Arch Street becoming a sanctuary church, Hynicka says he has been getting calls from churches across the country, seeking advice on how to do the same thing. "I can tell them how we

---

1   Kathy L. Gilbert, "United Methodist Churches Offer Sanctuary," UMC.org, January 23, 2017, http://www.umc.org/news-and-media /united-methodist-churches-offer-sanctuary.

have done things, but there are still things we haven't figured out," he said. "One of the things we haven't figured out yet and are constantly working on is maintaining a sense of security. There is no law that prevents ICE from coming into the church."

Garcia obtained an attorney to work on a strategy to get him a visa. "If you are a person simply undocumented and not connected to any advocacy organization or you don't have an attorney working for a possible path to getting a visa, it is a whole different ball game," Hynicka said.

On October 11, 2017, Javier Flores Garcia, a loving husband, father of three, and undocumented immigrant from Mexico, took his first steps in eleven months onto the pavement outside Arch Street Church. Garcia breathed the fresh air of freedom, accompanied by his family, attorney, and friends. Greeted by supporters with hugs, handshakes, and tears and by a gaggle of media, he was finally freed from fear of arrest and deportation by the federal Immigration and Customs Enforcement agency.

Garcia won his deportation case primarily because of the support of *Juntos*, a Latino immigrant community-led organization in Philadelphia. Juntos attorney Brennan Gian-Grasso said his client had been granted "deferred action," allowing him to live and work in the United States while awaiting approval of a visa.

"This was a love story," said Hynicka, celebrating the emancipation of his church's beloved sanctuary guest. "It was all about how the love of God, family, and community can lead to liberation."[2]

Biblical Reference

The call of Abram: "Go out from your land and from your kindred and go into the land that I will show you" (Acts 7:3 ESV). Abraham was a stranger and an alien in the land of Canaan (Genesis 23). Jacob moved his family to Egypt to escape the famine and reunite with Joseph (Gen 46:1-7). Joseph brought his Hebrew brothers to Pharaoh, and they were welcomed and given jobs (47:1-6).

Jesus: Jesus and his parents left his birthplace and hometown, fleeing to Egypt when Jesus was a baby to escape persecution (Matt 2:1-16, 19-23). There are at least two specific references to Jesus as an immigrant—the first practical, the second theological.

First the practical: Jesus was a Galilean and is referred to as such throughout the Gospels. Our modern conception of nation-states did not exist at the time of Jesus, nor did our modern conception of "immigrants." However, Jesus and his followers are identified throughout the Gospels as "Galileans" and had an outsider status in Jerusalem because they were from a client kingdom in the north. This was

> **Jesus and his followers had an outsider status in Jerusalem.**

---

2   John W. Coleman, "Phila. Church's 11-Month Sanctuary Guest Goes Home with Family," Eastern Pennsylvania Conference: The United Methodist Church website, October 13, 2017, https://www.epaumc.org/home-page/home-feature/2017/10/phila-churchs-11-month-sanctuary-guest-goes-home-with-family/.

not a positive association for the residents of Jerusalem. Based on his "outsider" geopolitical status, Jesus was thought of in Jerusalem similarly to how Mexican and other Latin American immigrants are thought of in the United States.

Now to the theological: we learn in the prologue to John's Gospel that "the Word became flesh and dwelt among us" (1:14 ESV). The Trinitarian's "Son's" experience is that of coming to dwell among humanity. This "dwelling among" might be faithfully rendered "immigrated to." We read in the prologue that "he was in the world, and the world came into being through him; yet the world did not know him. He came to what was his own, and his own people did not accept him" (John 1:10-11). Jesus' outsider or immigrant status is confirmed in that his people did not recognize him. God's identity in Jesus is as a stranger, an identity thrust upon him by those who do not recognize who he is. The divine is identified as an outsider, as an immigrant. Seeing Jesus Christ as an immigrant gives us a lens through which we see his action in Scripture.

Resource: Social Principle

[United Methodists] recognize, embrace, and affirm all persons, regardless of country of origin, as members of the family of God. We affirm the right of all persons to equal opportunities for employment, access to housing, health care, education, and freedom from social discrimination. We urge the Church and society to recognize the gifts, contributions, and struggles of those who are immigrants and to advocate for justice for all. We oppose immigration policies that separate family members from each other or that include detention of families with children, and we call on local churches to be in ministry with immigrant families. (*Book of Discipline 2016*, Social Principles, ¶162)

The General Board of Church and Society of The United Methodist Church calls upon all policy makers to work for just and compassionate migration policies that affirm the worth, dignity, and inherent value and rights of all persons regardless of nationality or legal status. (*The Book of Resolutions 2016*, #3281 "Welcoming the Migrant to the United States"):

> Supportive of churches offering sanctuary to migrants, Church and Society is especially concerned about the explicit targeting of communities determined to help those in need. Such policies are antithetical to the life and teaching of Jesus Christ and will not be celebrated as progress.

Sanctuary Guideline

The United Methodist Board of Church and Society, the denomination's social justice agency, gives guidelines to churches that want to become sanctuary churches. These guidelines are an ecumenical resource created and shared by many in the faith-based advocacy community. Jeania Ree Moore, director for civil and human rights for the agency, notes, "Many in immigrant communities are fearful of what changes the . . . president and administration will make that will impact their lives, livelihoods, and families." Moore also states, "While unpredictable, these threats are not unanticipated. Policy and practice under the Obama administration, along with new challenges under the Trump administration, have been prompting a proactive and broad response for years from concerned communities, faith and secular, immigrant and ally."[3]

The United Methodist Church's social agency has been supporting "Know Your Rights" sessions and engaging elected officials about standing in solidarity with the sojourner. Rev. Susan Henry-Crowe, top executive, says: "We are challenging a climate of fear with demonstration of welcome and love."[4]

The sanctuary movement is a growing movement of faith and immigrant communities doing what Congress and the administration refuse to do: protecting and standing with immigrants facing deportation. Members pledge to protect immigrant families who face workplace discrimination or deportation. United Methodists are joining the many religious leaders, congregations, and faith-based organizations of all denominations who are part of the movement.

Questions for Discussion

1. Think of a time when you felt welcomed by somebody when you were a stranger. How did that make you feel? What was it about the incident that made you feel welcomed?

2. How is your church welcoming to strangers? to recent immigrants?

3. What would you do if you encountered immigrants, and particularly undocumented immigrants, in your neighborhood? your church?

---

3 Gilbert, "United Methodist Churches Offer Sanctuary."
4 Gilbert.

Case Study 2: Hate Groups and White Supremacy

1. The Charleston Church Shooting

White Gunman Kills Nine African Americans at a Historic Black Church—June 17, 2015

"A heartbroken nation's tension turned to mourning . . . as news broke that the suspected gunman in . . . Charleston, South Carolina, . . . [was] arrested, and the identities of his nine victims were released," reported the *Huffington Post*.[5] The twenty-one-year-old gunman was said to have entered the Emanuel African Methodist Episcopal Church during a weekly Bible study and began shooting at 9 p.m. Six women and three men, including the church's pastor and state senator Clementa Pinckney, were killed.

Charleston Mayor Joe Riley said, "The only reason someone could walk into a church and shoot people praying is out of hate. It is the most dastardly act that one can possibly imagine."[6]

In a statement from the White House, then president Barack Obama mourned the victims and lamented the steady stream of mass shootings that had occurred while he was in office. "Once again, innocent people were killed in part because someone who wanted to inflict harm had no trouble getting their hands on a gun." Obama said, "At some point, we as a country will have to reckon with the fact that this type of mass violence doesn't happen in other . . . countries."[7]

---

5   Kelly Chen, "Charleston Church Shooting: White Gunman Kills 9 At Historic Black Church," *Huffington Post*, updated December 6, 2017, https://www.huffingtonpost.com/2015/06/17/charleston-shooting-churc_n_7608738.html,

6   Chen, "Charleston Church Shooting."

7   Chen, "Charleston Church Shooting."

2. Ferguson, Missouri

On August 9, 2014, Michael Brown, an unarmed black teen-ager, was shot and killed by Darren Wilson, a white police officer, in Ferguson, Missouri, a suburb of St. Louis. "The shooting prompted protests that roiled the area for weeks," reported the *New York Times*.[8]

A grand jury declined to indict Officer Darren Wilson in the fatal shooting of the unarmed black teen. The grand jury's decision meant that Wilson, twenty-eight, faced no state charges for the shooting of eighteen-year-old Brown. "It also set off a show of fury on streets near where Brown was shot," *Washington Post* writers added, "a reflection of emotions that registered in this riven city as either out of control or justifiable."[9] The article continues:

At least two police cars and a half-dozen buildings were set aflame. Not far from Christmas lights in downtown Ferguson that read "Seasons Greetings," police fired tear-gas canisters to contain the crowds. People looted liquor and convenience stores, a response that ran counter to the peace that Missouri

---

8   Larry Buchanan et al., "Q&A: What Happened in Ferguson?" the *New York Times*, updated August 10, 2015, https://www.nytimes .com/interactive/2014/08/13/us/ferguson-missouri-town-under -siege-after-police-shooting.html.
9   Quotations and details in this case study are taken from Chico Harlan, Wesley Lowery, and Kimberly Kindy, "Ferguson Police Officer Won't Be Charged in Fatal Shooting," *Washington Post*, November 25, 2014, https://www.washingtonpost.com/ politics/grand-jury-reaches-decision-in-case-of-ferguson -officer/2014/11/24/de48e7e4-71d7-11e4-893f-86bd390a3340_ story.html?utm_term=.393dc2c87a27.

authorities, President Obama and Brown's family had requested.

As St. Louis County Prosecuting Attorney Robert P. McCulloch announced the decision, National Guard troops fanned out across the city. There was calm and silence in the streets of Ferguson for a half-beat after the announcement, but anger erupted shortly thereafter, and just after midnight county police reported hearing automatic-weapon fire. Protestors also blocked Interstate 44, causing a miles-long back-up of traffic.

Four months later, the US Justice Department asked Ferguson to "overhaul its criminal justice system, declaring that the city had engaged in . . . constitutional violations."[10]

Biblical Reference

"Bear fruit worthy of repentance." (Matt 3:8)

"Beware of false prophets, who come to you in sheep's clothing but inwardly are ravenous wolves. You will know them by their fruits. Are grapes gathered from thorns, or figs from thistles? In the same way, every good tree bears good fruit, but the bad tree bears bad fruit. A good tree cannot bear bad fruit, nor can a bad tree bear good fruit. Every tree that does not bear good fruit is cut down and thrown

---

10 Matt Apuzzo and John Eligon, "Ferguson Police Tainted by Bias, Justice Department Says," the *New York Times*, March 4, 2015. https://www.nytimes.com/2015/03/05/us/us-calls-on-ferguson -to-overhaul-criminal-justice-system.html.

into the fire. Thus you will know them by their fruits." (Matt 7:15–20)

Happy are those who observe justice, who do righteousness at all times. (Ps 106:3)

Social Principle

We affirm all persons as equally valuable in the sight of God. We therefore work toward societies in which each person's value is recognized, maintained, and strengthened. We deplore acts of hate or violence against groups or persons based on race, color, national origin, ethnicity, age, gender, disability, status, economic condition, sexual orientation, gender identity or religious affiliation. . . .

Rights of Racial and Ethnic Persons—Racism is the combination of the power to dominate by one race over the races and a value system that assumes that the dominant race is innately superior to the others. Racism includes both personal and institutional racism. Personal racism is manifested through the individual expressions, attitudes, and/or behaviors that accept the assumptions of a racist value system and that maintain the benefits of this system. Institutional racism is the established social pattern that supports implicitly or explicitly the racist value system. Racism, manifested as sin, plagues and hinders our relationship with Christ, inasmuch as it is antithetical to the gospel itself. In many cultures white persons are granted unearned privileges and benefits that are denied to persons of color. We oppose the creation of a racial hierarchy in any culture. Racism breeds racial discrimination. We define racial discrimination as the disparate treatment and lack of full access and equity in resources, opportunities, and participation in the Church and in society based on race or ethnicity.

Therefore, we recognize racism as sin and affirm the ultimate and temporal worth of all persons. We rejoice in the gifts that particular ethnic histories and cultures bring to our total life. We commit as the Church to move beyond symbolic expressions and representative models that do not challenge unjust systems of power and access. (*Book of Discipline 2016*, Social Principles, ¶162)

Questions for Discussion

1. Think about your relationship with somebody in your family (a parent, sibling, brother/sister-in-law, grand-parent) or among your friends who has a background of Asian/Pacific Islander, Latino/a, Native American/indigenous to the Americas, African American, or of African or Anglo/white/European descent. How does that individual's background affect how other people treat him or her? How do you treat him or her?

2. Our upbringing, families, friends, schools, and churches, from which we develop our worldview, can be concealed by a monocultural perspective. Is this true in your experience?

3. What is your experience of racism? If you are of Anglo/white/European descent, how do you interact with racial-ethnic people? What is white privilege? Offer some examples.

4. How does denying the existence of racism and white privilege perpetuate racial inequality, segregation,

and miseducation? What helps in challenging racism? What doesn't help? What are the next steps?

5. What are some barriers within a faith community to building an inclusive community and overcoming racism?

6. What policies and/or procedures does your church or institution have to include people from other races and ethnicities?

Case Study 3: Poverty

Halima's Personal Story[11]

In early 2005, during the worst of the food crisis in Niger, Halima had to leave her village. "There was no food and I left my village of Sabarou, walking for 48 hours to the town of Dakoro. I had to spend the night on the road with my three children," she said.

She was fortunate to later find work cleaning houses in a nearby city. But Sabarou was home to Halima's community, and when Lutheran World Relief brought food to the village, the news traveled fast. All but two of 200 families who had abandoned the village in search of food and work had returned home by the day of distribution. Halima speaks of the impact of four years of failed harvests and the drain on her meager assets. She says the food would give the villagers strength to work in the upcoming harvest and help restore their sense of community.

---

11 The following is taken from the National Council of the Churches of Christ in the USA, *Eradicating Global Poverty: A Christian Study Guide on the Millennium Development Goals* (New York: National Council of the Churches of Christ in the USA, 2006), 15.

Biblical Reference

> Now while Jesus was at Bethany in the house of Simon the leper, a woman came to him with an alabaster jar of very costly ointment, and she poured it on his head as he sat at the table. But when the disciples saw it, they were angry and said, "Why this waste? For this ointment could have been sold for a large sum, and the money given to the poor." But Jesus, aware of this, said to them, "Why do you trouble the woman? She has performed a good service for me. For you always have the poor with you, but you will not always have me. By pouring this ointment on my body she has prepared me for burial. Truly I tell you, wherever this good news is proclaimed in the whole world, what she has done will be told in remembrance of her." (Matt 26:6-13)

> If a brother or sister is naked and lacks daily food, and one of you says to them, "Go in peace; keep warm and eat your fill," and yet you do not supply their bodily needs, what is the good of that? (James 2:15-16)

Resource: Poverty in the United States and Globally

The official poverty statistics are published by the United States Census Bureau. In a report issued in September 2017, the Bureau showed the following:[12]

- In 2016 there were 40.6 million people in poverty.

---

12 Jessica L. Semega, Kayla R. Fontenot, and Melissa A. Kollar, "Income and Poverty in the United States: 2016," September 2017, https://www.census.gov/content/dam/Census/library/publications/2017/demo/P60-259.pdf, 12, 14, 17, 18.

- The official poverty rate in 2016 was 12.7 percent.
- The 2016 poverty rate for blacks was 22.0 percent, for Hispanics 19.4 percent, and for Asians 10.1 percent. For non-Hispanic whites, the poverty rate was 8.8 percent.
- The poverty rate for children under eighteen was 18.0 percent in 2016, and the number of children in poverty was 13.3 million. Children represented 23.0 percent of the total population and 32.6 percent of people in poverty.
- Nearly 19 million Americans live in extreme poverty. This means their family's cash income is below one-half of their poverty threshold, or about $10,000 a year for a family of four. They represented 5.8 percent of all people and 45.6 percent of those in poverty.

Resource: Poverty in the World

The World Bank Group's mission, carved in stone at their Washington headquarters, states, "Our Dream is a World Free of Poverty." According to the World Bank website:

- This mission underpins all of the analytical, operational, and convening work in over 145 client countries, and is shored up by goals of bringing poverty to an end within a generation and promoting shared prosperity in a sustainable manner across the globe.
- In the past decades evidence shows a reduction of poverty. The first Millennium Development Goal target—to cut the 1990 poverty rate in half by 2015—was achieved five years ahead of schedule, in 2010. Despite the progress, the number of people still living in extreme poverty worldwide remains unacceptably

high. Considering forecasts, world poverty reduction may not be fast enough to reach the target of ending extreme poverty by 2030.[13]

- According to estimates at the time of their report, nearly 11 percent of the world's population were living on less than US $1.90 a day—approaching 770 million people. Worse, those in extreme poverty "often live in fragile contexts and remote areas. Access to good schools, healthcare, electricity, safe water and other critical services remains elusive."[14]

Questions for Discussion

1. Think about a time when you or someone you know had to manage life with limited resources. How did that make you feel? Talk about how that experience shaped your perspective about life.
2. What is a crucial difference between being poor and the kind of poverty that kills?
3. Jesus said the poor will always be with us (Matt 26:11). As a Christian, how do you feel about our ability to meet the challenge of eradicating extreme poverty? Consider how some children live in places you, your family, and/or your church support.
4. Reflect on the following questions:
   - What is the under-five mortality rate in your country or region?

---

13 The World Bank, "Poverty: Overview," World Bank Group website, last updated April 11, 2018, http://www.worldbank.org /en/topic/poverty/overview.

14 World Bank.

- What is the mortality rate for new mothers in your country or region?
- What are the social and traditional roles for boys and for girls in your family?
- For a country struggling with HIV/AIDS, how have children's lives been altered?

Case Study 4: The Intersection of Racism and Sexism

"How did we get the woman and how did they get the man?" exclaimed Mrs. Smith with frustration. Rev. Latasha Warner sat, not knowing how to respond, in front of the members of the Staff Parish Relations Committee (SPRC). Today was the day the district superintendent was introducing her to Mercy United Methodist Church. Their first female pastor, a Caucasian woman, had just been appointed elsewhere, and Reverend Warner was the new pastor. She would also be the first racial-ethnic pastor appointed to the church. Her husband, Rev. Raymond Warner, also a UMC pastor, had been appointed to Grace UMC, located about two miles away from Mercy UMC. Grace had also never had a racial-ethnic clergyperson.

Mercy and Grace UMCs shared a few relatives and friends in the same community, Ashville, so even before she was introduced to Mercy UMC, Reverend Warner had heard through the grapevine that members from both churches were murmuring, wondering if the conference was "browning" their churches. Ashville was changing rapidly, with more African Americans moving into the community, and the churches were becoming more integrated. She'd also heard that leaders of Mercy UMC were questioning why they had to receive a racial-ethnic woman pastor even though they had been paying their apportionment faithfully for years. They wondered what they had done wrong to receive not just a woman, but a racial-ethnic woman pastor.

The district superintendent told Reverend Warner that Mercy UMC could barely afford a minimum salary with the support from the annual conference. This meant that she would have the same salary for the next five years. She did not argue; however, she knew that the previous pastor had received much more than a minimum salary and that Mercy UMC was able to afford it.

She did not feel welcomed by the members of the SPRC. There was not much explanation about the reason and purpose of this appointment to the SPRC from the district superintendent either.

Suddenly, another member chimed in: "You are too authoritarian."

Reverend Warner was puzzled again, thinking, *I've only said a few words. You don't even know me, so why would you say that I am too authoritarian?* She understood that it would take a while for the congregation of the Mercy UMC to get to know her and accept her as their senior pastor, but she also wondered whether the SPRC members would have responded the same if she were at least a man.

Questions for Discussion

1. Does this case study ring true in your experience? What do you believe the SPRC members were thinking? What is the first thing Reverend Warner should do?
2. What would you do differently if you were a member of the SPRC at Mercy UMC?
3. How could the district superintendent be helpful to the SPRC at Mercy UMC?

Resources: Racial Inclusiveness and Gender

Inclusiveness of the Church—The United Methodist Church is a part of the church universal, which is one Body in Christ. The United Methodist Church acknowledges that all persons are of sacred worth. All persons without regard to race, color, national origin, status, or economic condition, shall be eligible to attend its worship services, participate in its programs, receive the sacraments, upon baptism be admitted as baptized members, and upon taking vows declaring the Christian faith, become professing members in any local church in the connection. In The United Methodist Church no conference or other organizational unit of the Church shall be structured so as to exclude any member or any constituent body of the Church because of race, color, national origin, status or economic condition. (*Book of Discipline 2016*, Article IV)

Women and Men—We affirm with Scripture the common humanity of male and female, both having equal worth in the eyes of God. We reject the erroneous notion that one gender is superior to another, that one gender must strive against another, and that members of one gender may receive love, power, and esteem only at the expense of another. We especially reject the idea that God made individuals as incomplete fragments, made whole only in union with another. We call upon women and men alike to share power and control, to learn to give freely and to receive freely, to be complete and to respect the wholeness of others. We seek for every individual opportunities and freedom to love and be loved, to seek and receive justice, and to practice ethical self-determination. We understand our gender diversity to be a gift from God, intended to add to the rich variety of human experience and perspective; and we guard against attitudes and traditions that would use this good gift to leave members of one sex more vulnerable in relationships than members of another. (*Book of Discipline 2016*, ¶161.F)

Jung Ha Kim and Rosetta Ross, *The Status of Racial and Ethnic Minority Clergywomen in The United Methodist Church.* (Nashville: General Board of Higher Education and Ministry, 2004.) https://www.gbhem.org/sites/default/files/documents /clergywomen/CW_RACIALETHNICSTUDY2004.PDF.

Case Study 5: Understanding Differences in Language

Pastor Lee was diligent about visiting her parishioners at home and at the hospital. She had learned about the importance of visitation while growing up in a church at home in South Korea. Her congregation recognized the change of pastoral care and appreciated having the experience of pastoral visitation.

One day, Pastor Lee went to see Harry Richardson, who was recuperating from surgery. When she arrived at the hospital, he was sitting in the recovery room. As soon as Pastor Lee entered the room, she said, "Oh, Harry, you look grouchy!"

Harry responded, "Pastor Lee, please do not make me laugh. I cannot laugh right now. Did you mean to say, 'You look groggy'?"

Pastor Lee laughed out loud. "I am sorry, Harry. Yes, I intended to say you look groggy."

Pastor Lee had come to Clinton United Methodist Church as a pastor in charge a year ago. She is the first racial-ethnic pastor in the history of the church, which is 150 years old. The church is located in Clinton, which is in a metropolitan area. It used to be a white majority community; however, the demographics of the area have been changing in recent years, and Clinton UMC is the only church in the community that is still an all-white congregation.

Ironically, it is also the only church that has a racial-ethnic pastor. Members of Clinton UMC drive into the city from suburbs to attend their church on Sundays.

Pastor Lee immigrated to the United States about ten years ago as a student. She felt that God was calling her to a cross-racial and cross-cultural ministry. If anybody asked about her call, Reverend Lee would respond, "My call is to be a bridge between two different cultures as an ordained minister."

Even though she speaks English fairly well, Reverend Lee is conscious of her accent. On Sundays, she provides a manuscript of her sermon for those who have told her that they could not understand her English. She was intimidated by those comments and felt discouraged serving an English-speaking congregation.

Pastor Lee prayed for Harry's quick recovery, and he was grateful for her visit. But as she was leaving the hospital, Pastor Lee wondered about how her speaking English as a second language impacts the ministry of Clinton UMC.

Questions for Discussion

1. What kinds of opportunities does Clinton UMC have by having Pastor Lee as their minister, someone who speaks English as a second language?

2. How does language shape who we are? What are some English phrases that cannot be adequately translated? Is it possible that some languages contain words or expressions that convey ideas or experiences in new or more expansive ways? How might knowing a different language deepen our understanding of who God is and by what name we call God?

3. What are the possible steps for a church to move forward with having a clergy whose English is a second language in the midst of increasing diversity among clergy?

Resources: Language and Leadership

The Committee, through the Board of Ordained Ministry, shall seek ways to make reasonable accommodations for cultural and ethnic/racial realities and language translations as candidates meet the requirement for candidacy, including interviews, psychological assessments, criminal background, and credit checks. (*Book of Discipline 2016*, ¶666.4)

Andy Molinsky, *Global Dexterity: How to Adapt Your Behavior Across Cultures without Losing Yourself in the Process*. (Boston: Harvard Business Review Press, 2013.)

Case Study 6: Working Collaboratively and Internationally with Differences in Race and Culture

Glen Adams shook his head as he hung up the phone. The call had come from one of the fifteen clergy going on a study tour he was organizing. The caller wanted to know the details of the trip itinerary, but Glen could not give more detailed information other than what he had already shared with the group. He had been trying to plan the trip for more than a year. It was now about a month before the trip, and he still didn't have a set agenda with detailed information for the trip other than regional and organization names with TBAs.

If it were solely dependent upon him, he would have everything planned by now. However, he had to work with several people from the country they were visiting to put the schedule together—including school officials, church leaders, and community leaders in that country. Communication with these leaders was spotty. Glen would send emails and not receive responses from those who were supposed to help him plan the trip. It would take a few weeks, with several reminders, to get responses. Sometimes the local leaders told him that their internet was not working.

Fifteen clergy who planned to go on the trip with Glen were eager to have more detailed information. After all, all of them were from North America, and their cultural managerial practice was to try their best to avoid uncertainty; they were used to timeliness, correct documents, and working with organized schedules. Glen was concerned that the participants would evaluate his performance as ineffective although he felt that his hands were tied under the circumstances. Glen is a racial-ethnic leader who functions well within a European American cultural framework. Nevertheless, he is conscious of the stereotype of racial-ethnic leaders regarding "timeliness" and "orderliness" in the North American culture.

As The UMC becomes more diverse and reaches out to a global community, Glen, in his role as a denominational administrator, has been increasingly involved with leaders outside of the United States. However, communication with these leaders has been difficult, especially around handling administrative details in a timely manner. Sometimes, it is an issue of language differences; other times it is a matter of different understandings of "timeliness," depending on the culture. Glen even experienced trip agenda changes once he arrived in the country. He usually reminds people who travel with him to be flexible and play it by ear when they go to a different country.

Generally, North Americans want to avoid uncertainty, and they get frustrated if they do not have the information in advance. Glen tried to explain that to the local leaders in the country they were to visit. During one of the trips, he tried his best to get detailed information about what was going to happen—and when—from a local leader, but the leader simply comforted Glen by telling him to relax and rest assured that everything would be all right. The leader also explained how it is almost impossible to tell what time the travelers would get there and when to start the next program because there are so many variables regarding road conditions in his country. Glen finally learned not to put exact times and instead listed what was going to happen during morning, afternoon, and evening. However, this does not resolve his concern of being viewed as an effective leader through the lens of North American culture.

Glen loves his work and understands that working with a global community is a noble effort. However, he often feels that he is caught in the middle between the Western/North American culture and the rest of the cultures in terms of management and administration. Sometimes he feels helpless. Glen wonders how we can work together effectively as global citizens and whether that is actually possible.

Questions for Discussion

1. What is the value of working across the globe? Please share some examples of working with people in different countries. What are the myths and what are the realities?
2. What is one thing that Glen can do to get where he wants to be regarding efficient administration?
3. What keeps getting in the way of honest conversation in a cross-racial and cross-cultural context?
4. How do different cultures deal with issues related to time?

Resources: Culture and Leadership

Racial Justice—The United Methodist Church proclaims the value of each person as a unique child of God and commits itself to the healing and wholeness of all persons. The United Methodist Church recognizes that the sin of racism has been destructive to its unity throughout its history. Racism continues to cause painful division and marginalization. The United Methodist Church shall confront and seek to eliminate racism, whether in organizations or in individuals, in every facet of its life and in society at large. The United Methodist Church shall work collaboratively with others to address concerns that threaten the cause of racial justice at all times and in all places. (*Book of Discipline 2016*, Article V)

David Livermore, *Leading with Cultural Intelligence: The Real Secret to Success*. (New York: AMACOM, 2015).

2

Leadership Theories in Cross-Racial and Cross-Cultural Contexts

The goal of this chapter is to reflect on leadership theories as they relate to cross-racial and cross-cultural contexts. Understanding the results of empirical research about effective leadership will help us work together, consider global trends, and avoid mistakenly thinking that a leader from a different culture is simply ineffective just because he or she leads differently. The question we consider in this chapter is, what is effective leadership from a global perspective?

The Global Leadership and Organizational Behavior Effectiveness organization (GLOBE) conducted a study affirming that there is a set of leadership qualities that the global community upholds. The GLOBE study also reminds us that there are *culturally endorsed implicit theories of leadership* (CLT) in each culture.[1] These common values constitute what effective leadership is and what it is not in a particular culture. In cross-racial and cross-cultural contexts, we often judge a leader who is from a different culture based

---

1   Robert J. House et al., eds., *Culture, Leadership, and Organizations: The GLOBE Study of 62 Societies* (Thousand Oaks, CA: Sage Publications, 2004).

on our own CLT. In other words, culture plays a strong role in how we perceive the content of leaders' attributes and behaviors; and consequently, we decide whether or not these leaders are desirable and effective by the standards of our own culture.[2] Unfortunately, ethnocentrism and prejudice are usually involved in this process of evaluating a leader from a different culture. For example, we may quickly conclude that leaders are ineffective based on our cultural understanding of how communication should be dealt with.

Eric H. F. Law, founder and executive director of the Kaleidoscope Institute, explains that prejudice is when we judge others based on self-oriented values and attitudes. If individuals express their prejudice through an action, it becomes discrimination. If discrimination is systematic or system-wide, it becomes racism.[3] He goes on to say that ethnocentrism is a belief that one's cultural values and beliefs are the norms against which all others are measured. For example, in North America "timeliness" or the tendency to plan ahead and deliver on time is one measure of leadership effectiveness. But different cultures have different understandings of what constitutes timeliness and what is considered being "on time."

> Culture plays a strong role in how we perceive the content of leaders' attributes and behaviors.

Is there a leadership theory that is particularly helpful in cross-racial and cross-cultural contexts? A theory that will minimize the effects of culture bias? And how is leadership in

---

2   House et al., 672.
3   Eric H. F. Law, *The Bush Was Blazing but Not Consumed* (St. Louis: Chalice Press, 1996).

cross-racial and cross-cultural contexts different from leadership in a monocultural context, especially if "leadership is culturally contingent"?[4] The answer can be that leading people in cross-racial and cross-cultural contexts is a calling, and people can learn the needed skills. In other words, leadership is a dynamic expression of a leader's learned beliefs, values, and attitudes; yet leadership comes from the whole person—one's intellect, heart, spirit, and relationships with self, others, and God.

> Leading people in cross-racial and cross-cultural contexts is a calling, and people can learn the needed skills.

A well-known leadership scholar, Peter G. Northouse, defined leadership this way: "Leadership is a process whereby an individual influences a group of individuals to achieve a common goal."[5] For example, the common goal in cross-racial and cross-cultural ministry is to create an alternative human community where individuals can learn from each other's differences with respect, which comes out of their faith in Jesus Christ, who commands us to love one another. Loving someone who is different from oneself is not a typical or natural phenomenon. John Bunyan in 1680 said, "Birds of a feather flock together," which means that people who have the same interest and perspective naturally are attracted to each other. It takes intentionality to go beyond simple curiosity about "otherness." A leader in this context is a person of influence who seeks to genuinely

---

4   Law, 5.
5   Northouse and Lee, *Leadership Case Studies in Education*, loc. 143 (see introduction, n. 1).

love someone in spite of differences by sharing ideas and practicing what he or she believes. It takes a commitment to love someone "in spite of." This is why it is a good idea to establish a covenant concerning how to relate to each other between leader and followers in a cross-racial and cross-cultural context.

Global Attributes of an Effective Leader

What constitutes effective leadership from a global perspective? The GLOBE Project "empirically identified leadership attributes that are universally perceived as contributors to or inhibitors of outstanding leadership."[6] This study identified twenty-one implicit leadership qualities that contribute to effective leadership worldwide. A leader is trustworthy, just, honest (has integrity), encouraging, positive, dynamic, confidence-building, motivational (charismatic-inspirational), communicative, informed, dependable, intelligent, decisive, administratively skilled, and excellence-oriented. This kind of leader exercises foresight, plans ahead (charismatic-visionary), and is a coordinator, team builder, motive arouser, effective bargainer, and win-win problem solver.[7]

Let's take another look at "timeliness." The GLOBE study said that "timeliness" is connected to an "uncertainty avoidance" orientation. Uncertainty avoidance is "the extent to which a society, organization, or group relies on social norms, rules, and procedures to alleviate unpredictability of future events."[8] The study shows that the tendency toward "uncertainty avoidance" correlates to individual societal

---

6   House et al., *Culture, Leadership, and Organizations*, 670.
7   House et al., 677.
8   House et al., 30.

health and general satisfaction. Those who feel satisfied with their social context engage more future-oriented behaviors with planning and investment.[9] The authors also provide an illustration that shows the grand means of GLOBE societal practices and societal values scales for Uncertainty Avoidance across all GLOBE societies: "The average of societal Uncertainty Avoidance practices across 61 countries is 4.16, and the range is 2.88 to 5.37. The mean value falls on the midpoint of 4.0 on a scale of 1 to 7."[10] This means, in a global context, that an effective leader is a person who tends to avoid uncertainty and plans ahead for the future.

The study also identified six leadership styles that contribute to effective global leadership:[11]

1. *Charismatic/value-based leadership.* A leader practicing this style of leadership is visionary, inspirational, self-sacrificing, decisive, and performance-oriented, and has integrity.

2. *Team-oriented leadership.* This kind of leadership helps a team work together so that they can implement a common goal.

3. *Participative leadership.* This leadership style reflects a leader's ability to include others in the decision-making process. This means that the leader is not autocratic.

4. *Humane-oriented leadership.* A leader practicing this leadership style demonstrates modesty and has an ability to care for others.

---

9   House et al., 38.
10 House et al., 621, table 19, 620.
11 House et al., 14.

5. *Autonomous leadership.* This leadership style is demonstrated by leaders having individual and unique leadership attributes.

6. *Self-protective leadership.* With this leadership style, the leader is protective of the group's safety and security by preserving members' honor.

The GLOBE project concluded that the most effective global leader is one who has integrity, charisma, and interpersonal skills. But an effective *global* leader is also one who is sensitive to power differentials—reducing the gap between the less powerful and the more powerful, the "power distance."[12] These leaders not only pay attention to how their power is exercised, but they also exhibit a high level of performance orientation.[13]

Adaptive Leadership

In 2014, I conducted a survey in collaboration with Mark McCormack at the General Board of Higher Education and Ministry (GBHEM) of The United Methodist Church on the leadership style of United Methodist racial-ethnic lead pastors serving cross-racial and cross-cultural appointments. The vision of GBHEM is to develop "generations of thriving, diverse, and compassionate Christian leaders for The United Methodist Church and the world."[14]

---

12 Mauk Mulder, *The Daily Power Game* (New York: Springer, 2012); Geert Hofstede, *Culture's Consequences* (Thousand Oaks, CA: Sage Publications, 2001).

13 Northouse and Lee, *Leadership Case Studies in Education*, locs. 2227–64.

14 HiRho Park, "Leadership Style of UMC Racial-Ethnic Lead Pastors Who Are Serving Cross-Racial and Cross-Cultural Appointments," GBHEM.org, September 24, 2014, https://www.gbhem

The 2014 study was a comparison study that I conducted with Susan Willhauck about the leadership style of clergy-women who are serving large churches with one thousand or more members.[15] In this study racial-ethnic lead pastors were considered those who are serving Caucasian-majority churches with five hundred or more members. One of the distinguishing attributes of these pastors was adaptability. Adaptive leaders are fluent and versatile, willing to take a risk and start new things. They are socially and contextually conscientious about enabling a living faith while bringing diverse people together and closer to God as disciples of Christ. They practice a dialectical relationship between the Word of God and Christian practice, which mirrors John Wesley's formula for discipleship formation. They continue to learn and develop their leadership skills and participate in the formation of a self. The survey witnesses to the fact that racial-ethnic cross-racial and cross-cultural (RE CR-CC) lead pastors are adaptive leaders with the skills necessary to serve cross-racial and cross-cultural appointments.

According to Ronald Heifetz and his coauthors, in their *The Practice of Adaptive Leadership*, adaptive leadership is "the practice of mobilizing people to tackle tough challenges and thrive" with persistence.[16] It involves four key activities.

.org/sites/default/files/documents/clergy/Clergy_Leadership Style_HiRho2014.pdf.

15 HiRho Y. Park and Susan Willhauck, eds., *Breaking Through the Stained Glass Ceiling: Women Pastoring Large Churches* (Nashville: General Board of Higher Education and Ministry, 2013).

16 Ronald Heifetz, Alexander Grashow, and Marty Linsky, *The Practice of Adaptive Leadership: Tools and Tactics for Changing Your Organization and the World* (Boston: Harvard Business Press, 2009), loc. 414, Kindle.

- First, adaptive leaders observe events and see patterns.
- Second, adaptive leadership focuses on process.
- Third, an adaptive leader listens and takes time trying to diagnose the situation as opposed to imposing a quick fix.

Diagnosing the context is an essential element of adaptive leadership.[17] An adaptive leader asks what it takes to thrive in a new and challenging environment. This is a crucial leadership quality in cross-racial and cross-cultural contexts. Then an adaptive leader holds multiple interpretations of the situation by including different perspectives, which correlates to the participative leadership from the GLOBE study. More than 32 percent of RE CR-CC lead pastors "always" lead change by equipping others, and 28.6 percent of RE CR-CC lead pastors "often and always" make decisions by taking a vote, compared to 1.1 percent of white lead pastors in large churches.

- Fourth, an adaptive leader designs strategies based on observations and interpretations to tackle identified challenges, so that a faith community or organization will thrive in a new environment.[18] For example, of the RE CR-CC lead pastors asked, 59.5 percent reported that their leadership style changed or shifted emphasis since they had moved into a new, large-membership-church context. In addition, if we look at the career trajectories, these pastors are the ones who can take challenges in different settings

---

17 Heifetz, Grashow, and Linsky, 32.
18 Heifetz, Grashow, and Linsky, 32.

accordingly: 10.5 percent of RE CR-CC lead pastors have served as chairs of the Board of Ordained Ministry; 7.9 percent served a ministry outside of a local church; and 23.3 percent have been associate pastors. Moreover, almost half of RE CR-CC lead pastors are second-career pastors.[19]

Authentic Leadership

Bill George, in his book *Authentic Leadership*, notes that the single most important characteristic a leader should possess is "authenticity."[20] George argues that understanding "being the person you were created to be" is the most important trait for being an authentic leader. Knowing "who one is" is an invaluable trait of an effective leader, especially in a cross-racial and cross-cultural context.

According to George, an authentic leader is not born but develops over a lifetime.[21] Sixty-eight percent of RE CR-CC lead pastors said that they are conscious of developing leadership skills based on their life experiences as a racial-ethnic minority in US society and the career skills they have learned through the years (see page 11).

Authentic leaders understand the purpose of their leadership.

> Authentic leaders understand the purpose of their leadership.

19 Park, "Leadership Style of UMC Racial-Ethnic Lead Pastors Who Are Serving Cross-Racial and Cross-Cultural Appointments," 5.
20 Bill George, *Authentic Leadership: Rediscovering the Secrets to Creating Lasting Value* (San Francisco: Jossey-Bass, 2003), loc. 227, Kindle.
21 George, loc. 237.

They recognize the value and impact of their leadership to the community. They understand the importance of relationship building between leaders and followers. They are consistent and committed to self-discipline. They lead from the heart as their own individual persons.

According to Rita Nakashima Brock, self-construction, which refers to the constant improvising of self by embracing the "both-and" fluidity of a pluralistic culture and maintaining a strong sense of self at the same time, is a key to authentic leadership. Brock calls this process "interstitial integrity." The word *interstitial* originated from *interstitium*, tissue that connects the organs in the human body.[22] Brock's concept of "interstitial integrity" appeals to a need for the church to fulfill its role of bringing people together in the midst of multifaceted perspectives, ideas, and religious preferences. Brock, who is a Japanese Peruvian theologian, said "interstitial integrity" represents racial-ethnic people's image of self-construction, again referring to the constant formation of self in the midst of diverse cultural influences.

W. E. B. Du Bois, a sociologist, historian, and social activist, expressed the negotiating process of finding an authentic self as an African American in US society by introducing the term *double consciousness* in his book *The Souls of Black Folk* (1903). "Double consciousness" is a journey that an individual goes through to find a clear identity in spite of being aware that he or she is understood through the perspectives of others in a society. Northouse defines authentic

---

22 Rita Nakashima Brock, "Cooking Without Recipes: Interstitial Integrity," in *Off the Menu: Asian and Asian North American Women's Religious Theology,* ed. Rita Nakashima Brock et al. (Louisville: Westminster John Knox Press, 2007), 126.

leadership as "transparent, morally grounded, and responsive to people's needs and values."[23]

An authentic leader in a cross-racial and cross-cultural context is one who has a clear self-awareness culturally, socially, and politically. This leader has the ability to embrace "both-and" cultural fluidity and exercises a people-centered leadership with integrity, meaning that he or she makes the needs of others a priority. For example, RE CR-CC lead pastors are creating their own authentic leadership styles by synthesizing their distinctive cluster of cultural ideas and theological understandings. For RE CR-CC lead pastors, being an authentic leader means being vulnerable; their presence and a different leadership style shatters ethnocentrism and opens up a new possibility among their followers. Their vulnerability challenges the congregation and many times leads them to a spiritual transformation toward a new and different future for the church.

> An authentic leader in a cross-racial and cross-cultural context is one who has a clear self-awareness culturally, socially, and politically.

As mentioned earlier, leadership is culturally contingent, and practicing leadership in cross-racial and cross-cultural contexts involves interaction with historical, social, political, and cultural diversity and rapidly evolving communication technology across the globe. In the midst of this pluralistic context, an effective leader must understand what it means to be a global leader.

---

23 Northouse and Lee, *Leadership Case Studies in Education*, loc, 1278.

Transformational Leadership

Leading in cross-racial and cross-cultural milieus is all about transformation. To create an alternative human community where individuals can "love one another" in spite of or because of differences means that members of a faith community or organization may have to transform how they see the world. There needs to be a shift in recognizing effective leadership apart from one's own *culturally endorsed implicit theories of leadership* (CLT).

According to Northouse, transformational leaders are "change agents who are good role models, can create and articulate a clear vision, empower followers to meet higher standards, act in ways that make others want to trust them, and give meaning to organizational life."[24] Bernard M. Bass articulated the characteristics of transformational leadership as follows: exhibiting a role modeling charisma, inspiring motivation, and having the ability to challenge and empower followers.[25] A transformational leader in cross-racial and cross-cultural contexts is an authentic leader who can be a strong role model, who can articulate why working across races and cultures is important, and, at the same time, challenges followers' beliefs and values so that they act differently.

One of the prime examples of being a transformational leader is South African activist and former president Nelson Mandela. His enduring resistance and peaceful protests challenged people to speak up for peace and justice. Mandela's leadership brought the end of apartheid in South

---

24 Northouse and Lee, locs., 1144–48.

25 Bernard M. Bass and Ronald E. Riggio, *Transformational Leadership* (Mahwah, NJ: Lawrence Erlbaum Associates, 2008), locs. 4157–58, Kindle.

Africa, and when he became the first African president in his country in 1994, he formed a multiethnic government. He never forgot who he was and where he came from even during twenty-seven years in prison, yet he brought whites and blacks together to create a new form of reconciling community in South Africa and beyond.

Transformational leadership happens where there is an interactive relationship between a leader and followers. The most important part of transformational leadership within a cross-racial and cross-cultural context is the constituency, or followers. This is why a transformational leader develops followers, so they will commit themselves to share a vision and the goals of an organization, inspired by the charisma of a leader.[26]

One example of a charismatic leader who raised grass-roots leadership focused on his vision is Barack Obama, the first African American president in the United States. According to the *New York Times*, Obama's presidential campaign especially mobilized young people, who helped raise more than $750 million, including unprecedented online donations. Obama's followers believed in his vision of bringing racial-ethnic people, particularly African Americans, and liberal whites together and thereby establishing a more inclusive and diverse American society regardless of age, race, ethnicity, gender, economic status, or sexuality. Obama's followers understood that his goals were meant for their benefit, not just for his ego. After all, transformational leadership happens in a communal setting, never isolated from the grass roots; transformational leadership is a communal process.

---

26 Bass and Riggio, locs. 174–211.

Bass emphasizes that the heart of the paradigm of transformational leadership is the empowerment of followers. Northouse also underlines that authentic leadership happens in groups.[27] Jesus is a prime example of a transformational leader. He called twelve disciples and empowered them to proclaim the good news (Matt 28:19; Mark 16:15). Jesus kept the "power distance" low between his followers and himself as a leader; "I am the vine, you are the branches," he told them. "Those who abide in me and I in them bear much fruit, because apart from me you can do nothing" (John 15:5).

So, how can the followers create a culture of transformational leadership? According to *The Practice of Adaptive Leadership,* a leader and his or her followers can create a culture of transformation. First, members of a community must be able to name the problems openly and honestly. Second, the followers need to share responsibility for the organization's future by participating in decision-making. Third, members should be able to exercise independent judgment by voicing authentic perspectives in their own voice. Fourth, followers need to keep developing their leadership capacity by continuously learning new knowledge and skills. Finally, followers need to intentionally institutionalize reflection with a leader.[28]

Effective leadership in cross-racial and cross-cultural settings requires authenticity, adaptability, and transformational qualities. It is a communal process rather than a demonstration and expression of individual leadership. Effective

---

27 Northouse and Lee, *Leadership Case Studies in Education,* loc. 1284.
28 Heifetz, Grashow, and Linsky, *The Practice of Adaptive Leadership,* locs. 365-86.

leaders in cross-racial and cross-cultural contexts practice leadership from the heart, locating the needs of people in the center of their decision-making. The leader's concern is to empower the grass roots, seeking justice and welfare for all. Leaders are conscious of different perspectives because they understand that the foundation of their leadership comes from who they are and who God intends them to be, making their leadership a witness of God's creation.

Questions for Discussion

1. Share a time when you met an authentic leader. What made that person authentic? What made people want to follow him or her?
2. Who is exercising adaptive leadership around you? What does it look like? What kind of results were achieved, and how?
3. Think of a time when you were a follower. What did or could you do to create a culture of transformational leadership?
4. What leadership style is the best fit for you as a leader? As a follower?
5. Thinking of your own leadership, what skills do you need to develop to be more effective?

3

Being a Faith Community

Robert J. Schreiter, in his book *The New Catholicity*, states that the task of the church in this global world is to interact with its changing contexts.[1] In the midst of cultural and religious pluralism, the church is called to be a new mode of being as a Christian community. In the contour of a global church, how can the church respect particularities of diverse leadership styles and cultural confluence within Christianity, while at the same time keeping its theological integrity and "catholic spirit"? Is there any Christian practice or set of practices that can help the church accomplish this task in a global context?

A People-Centered Church

Natalie K. Watson, in her book *Introducing Feminist Ecclesiology,* argues that historically, a church has been defined by what people believe about its institutional structure rather than by how people experience the church as a Christian

---

1   Robert J. Schreiter, *The New Catholicity: Theology between the Global and the Local* (Maryknoll, NY: Orbis, 1997).

faith community.[2] She asks, "Who is the church?"[3]–then suggests that it should be a space in which all people can flourish and celebrate that they are created in the image of the God.[4] For example, traditional understandings of church, based on hierarchical and patriarchal perspectives, are often experienced as marginalizing for women. Watson argues that a church that takes a wide range of human experiences seriously can instead become a place of empowerment for all people. From this perspective, the church can shift from "a site of marginalization" to "a site of empowerment" when people are encouraged to share their own stories.[5]

Jesus said, "I came that they [my sheep] may have life, and have it abundantly" (John 10:10). Jesus placed people and their need to live an abundant life in the center of his ministry. An abundant life begins by knowing God, which is "justification" and continues to be nurtured by responding to God's grace, "sanctification," throughout one's life.[6]

---

2   Natalie K. Watson, *Introducing Feminist Ecclesiology* (Cleveland: Pilgrim Press, 2002), 38.
3   Watson, 9.
4   Watson, 119.
5   Watson, 117.
6   For Wesleyans, God's "prevenient grace" is represented by baptism, and to affirm prevenient grace is also to affirm that the grace of God is freely given to everyone. "Renewing grace" liberates believers from the bondage of brokenness and restores them to the image of God through the process of sanctification. From this perspective, Wesley's concept of salvation requires our participation and thus makes it possible, so that we can refer to it, in the words of theologian Randy Maddox, as "responsible grace." Maddox is convinced that Wesley's concept of responsible grace is the key to his theological activity, enabling Christians to live through justification toward a life of transformation.

This is the way of perfection, according to Wesley's theology. Jesus was willing to die for this reason, providing abundant life to people regardless of their social status, education, class, gender, sexual orientation, cultural background, and political association.

Jesus was intentional about putting people's needs in the center of his ministry; and thus he also made a theological statement about God's grace. John Wesley's "practical divinity" likewise started with placing people and their need for salvation at the center of his mission and ministry. For Wesley, "holiness of life" is impossible unless an individual's life is transformed so that he or she can contribute toward making a difference in the community. Like the Confucian understanding of relationality, an individual's transformation ripples through a community, a society, a nation, and the world. Locating people at the center of church life involves faith practices, because the existence of humanity represents God's love, and human vessels hold an image of God within. The church affirms the embodiment of God's grace in baptism and confirms the image of God within each person as we share Holy Communion as a community.

Christians shape church tradition through practicing their faith, yet their faith is not fully alive until they learn to

---

This process is what Wesley called *sanctification*. As a "justified" person, one should pursue the holy life throughout his or her lifetime, a process Wesley called "Christian perfection." Wesley's understanding of perfection is not a state of arrival but a maturing, gradual work in Christians. Christians have a responsibility to hold each other accountable in "works of piety" and "works of mercy." Faith must bring forth good works as its fruits. Randy L. Maddox, ed., *Rethinking Wesley's Theology for Contemporary Methodism* (Nashville: Kingswood Books, 1998).

respond to human conditions of suffering with concrete actions. Wesley's words, "There is no holiness but social holiness", reveal this point.[7] As expressed in the Social Principles,[8] Wesleyans have historically been diligent about being a relevant church for an evolving society, which means being accountable to the needs of people in the world.

> Jesus was intentional about putting people's needs in the center of his ministry; and thus he also made a theological statement about God's grace.

The preamble of *The Book of Discipline of The United Methodist Church* describes the church as a constant "redeeming" organic community that responds to the world:

The church is a community of all true believers under the Lordship of Christ. It is the redeemed and redeeming fellowship in which the Word of God is preached by persons divinely called, and the sacraments are duly administered according to Christ's own appointment. Under the discipline of the Holy Spirit the church seeks to provide for the maintenance of worship, the edification of believers, and the redemption of the world. The church of Jesus Christ

---

7 Thomas Jackson, ed., *The Works of John Wesley* (Nashville: Providence House, 1995), 14:321, CD-ROM.

8 The Social Principles represent Methodist concern for "the human issues in the contemporary world from a sound biblical and theological foundation" that call "all members of The United Methodist Church to a prayerful, studied dialogue of faith and practice." *Book of Discipline 2016*, Part V, Social Principles, 105-6.

exists in and for the world, and its very dividedness is a hindrance to its mission in that world.[9]

It is clear that the church, as "a redeeming fellowship," is a fluid entity that should be able to bring the world's people to God through practices of mercy and justice imitating the ministry of Jesus, who intentionally addressed the needs of people and embraced them with God's grace. By doing so, Jesus created an alternative community, which is open to differences and enlightens people by showing that being a faith community is about caring for and empowering people, helping them fulfill their potential to live into God's reign by grace, not by keeping laws. The practice of locating people in the center of ministry prevents the church from being an exclusive community, because it continually redirects the church back to its core; that is, the church is there for God's people regardless of who they are. When a church is conscious about the value of people who both individually and corporately embody the grace of God, "otherness" becomes the cornerstone for building community. Therefore, the practices of the church to include others become its way of connecting people for ministry rather than creating confusion and dissent.

Understanding Otherness: A Point of Connection

How do people encounter otherness? "Othering" has been used since the beginning to form boundaries and identities. However, from God's perspective, "otherness" is a point of connection within God's creation, because it completes the holistic circle of creation by mirroring God's

___
9 *Book of Discipline 2016*, Part I, The Constitution, 25.

revelation. Because God is completely Other to us, we can see God in others through their otherness. In recognizing God's Otherness, we experience God's mystery and wonder. From recognizing the otherness of a stranger, we can experience the mystery and wonder of friendship, agape, compassion, humility, justice, mercy—the attributes of God enfleshed in Jesus Christ. From this perspective, in Christian faith otherness can become a point of connection—connection to God the Creator, Sustainer, Redeemer—to fellow sisters and brothers whom we experience as also created in God's image.

So the question arises, how should Christians engage others as we respond to the calling to be faithful in a context where the church engages the complexity of social and cultural diversity? When a church ignores the theological and philosophical value of otherness within the holistic perspective of creation and humanity, it rejects and excludes those who can help it become more Christlike and avoid causing unnecessary pain, confusion, and dissention among Christians.

But even in the church, engaging others is difficult. And when we ourselves experience being named "other," it offends us. It makes us feel excluded, unwanted, devalued. It shocks our system and pushes us to the edge of our comfort zone. In fact, it seems that people's natural, first reaction to being named "other" is resistance, drawing the line, confusion, or murmuring.

The politics of a new mode of being the church in a global context is to build relationships among people in more effective ways. In other words, Christians are called to be bridge builders, which requires openness to learning from one another through dialogue and willingness to acknowledge that otherness is a part of God's revelation, despite our possible discomfort. By doing so, Christian bridge builders create a space for all people by constantly improvising permeable boundaries to embrace a both-and identity in a pluralistic culture and thus finding another side of themselves.

The ethics of bridge builders is expressed through the virtues of patience, listening, and respect, all fortified by love and the grace of God, as Jesus demonstrated in his ministry. When the virtue of respect is absent, tokenism becomes prevalent as a way of inclusion. The practice of being a bridge builder demands specific actions. Jesus was both human and divine, so as such, he took on the burden of Otherness, and consequently extended the boundary of God's realm to the world by being the Bridge Builder, the point of connection himself. While we are only human, we nonetheless can count on the power of the Holy Spirit to help us.

A church that embraces the Otherness of God finds itself articulating what it means to get along with one another in spite of differences of gender, culture, and ideology under the lordship of Jesus Christ. A people-centered church is a fellowship of redeemed and redeeming people where human suffering is released through dialogue, exchange of ideas, and sharing of faith, without feeling guilt or rejection. If the church is a community of the faithful—not just a building—its mode of being can be realized by weaving, through Christian faith, otherness with a deep appreciation and respect for humanity.

Being a Faith Community: A *Han*-Releasing Church (*Han-Puri Madang*)

The Spirit of the Lord is upon me, because he has anointed me to bring good news to the poor. He has sent me to proclaim release to the captives and recovery of sight to the blind, to let the oppressed go free, to proclaim the year of the Lord's favor. (Luke 4:18-19)

Every human being has afflictions in life, and often they are directly connected to the social, economic, cultural, and political context where we live. For example, classism, sexism, ageism, homophobia, and cultural imperialism—all of these experiences affect the human psyche, and we silently suffer from pains and wounds that leave scars deep in our hearts and souls. In Korean, this kind of human suffering is called *han*. A Korean theologian, Chang-Hee Son, defines *han* as "an affliction of a heart and struggle with a deep emotional or spiritual pain."[10] *Han* is the multilayered social and political suffering that prevents the community or individuals from realizing their full potential as holistic creatures of God.

God is our liberator. From this perspective, Christ is seen as a priest of *han,* the One who consoles the brokenhearted, heals the afflicted, and restores wholeness through communication with the divine. For God to be the liberator through Jesus Christ, people need a safe, trustful space where they can release their *han*, and a Christian faith community can be a such a space.

---

10 Chang-Hee Son, *Haan of Minjung Theology and Han of Han Philosophy: In the Paradigm of Process Philosophy and Metaphysics of Relatedness* (Lanham, MD: University Press of America, 2000), 4.

In Korean culture, *han-puri madang* is an open space for people to come together to release their *han*. It is an ancient Korean tradition that provides an emancipatory space for people in the midst of Korean society, and it is Koreans' unique ritual of untangling or releasing their deep pain. In this open space, people gather together and release their *han* as they go through rituals consisting of dialogue, singing, and dance. *Madang* is also a radical space where people can see the light of a new reality by practicing *han-puri*. *Han-puri madang* is a catalyst for people to express the otherness that caused their suffering without feeling threatened by government hierarchy. The *han-puri madang* is still practiced in Korea among younger generations, especially when they demonstrate their concerns against the government.

> For God to be the liberator through Jesus Christ, people need a safe, trustful space where they can release their *han*, and a Christian faith community can be a such a space.

Contemporary theologians Stanley Hauerwas and Avery Dulles, along with the founder of Methodism, John Wesley, all agree that the church should be able to read the "signs of the times." According to Hauerwas, the church should be a "distinctive people formed by the narrative of God."[11] "Distinctive people" refers to Christians who witness Christ to the world through practices of faith. Likewise, John Wesley emphasized the church being a community that holds

---

11 Stanley Hauerwas, "The Servant Community: Christian Social Ethics," in *The Hauerwas Reader,* ed. John Berkman and Michael Cartwright (Durham: Duke University Press, 2001), 371.

together "personal assurance and social witness, personal holiness and social holiness, holiness of heart and holiness of life."[12] Wesley said, "Christianity is essentially a social religion, and . . . to turn it into a solitary one is to destroy it."[13] For Wesley the church as a community meant a gathering of a critical mass of faithful Christians who take their personal and social responsibilities seriously.

Wesley's commitment to addressing people's *han* in his own practice of faith stemmed from his transforming religious experience at Aldersgate Street in London in 1738. This experience became foundational to his spirituality. It helped him understand, at a personal level, that God's work of salvation is free for all through God's grace, as the scripture says, "For by grace you have been saved through faith, and this is not your own doing; it is the gift of God—not the result of works, so that no one may boast" (Eph 2:8-9).[14] Over time, Wesley's understanding of church evolved from strictly being an institution to understanding it to be a "redeeming fellowship" for all people; therefore, he was not afraid of risking rejection when practicing his faith. Wesley preached on the street and in the fields; he allowed women to speak at Christian gatherings; he advocated against child and slave labor; and he taught about money, which is still not an easy subject to talk about. He encouraged Methodists to earn,

---

12 Jack A. Keller Jr., "The Church as a Community of Moral Discourse," in United Methodism and American Culture, Volume 3: Doctrines and Discipline, ed. Dennis M. Campbell, William B. Lawrence, and Russell E. Richey (Nashville: Abingdon Press, 1999), 215.

13 Jackson, *The Works of John Wesley*, 5:296.

14 Prevenient grace "surrounds all humanity and precedes any and all of our conscious impulses." *Book of Discipline 2016*, ¶102, 52.

save, and give as much as they can. All of these were new ministries and a result of placing the needs of people at the center of his ministry.

Wesley's emphasis on the integration of "works of piety" and "works of mercy" provides a creative tension between spiritual formation and practical love for a church with an open space available for all.[15] Wesley's emphasis on the dialectical relationship between faith and works, love and reason, individual and society, small group ("class" system) and community solidarity, and practice and theory is a way of expressing how God's grace is revealed in the totality of Christian spirituality and Christian practice in an everyday, concrete life.

As global citizens we witness people's experience of *han* or we have witnessed collective *han,* such as violence caused by racism or the death of loved ones due to terrorism. These tragedies deepen our spirituality as Christians; sometimes we question God, our faith, and what it means to live this life. But they also can lead us to become conscientious about practicing an inclusive model of ministry by placing people and their needs in the center of our concern. We can encounter "holiness in life" as we suffer together with wounded people; and we can more fully experience God, who suffers with humanity while releasing the power of grace that empowers Christians with a capacity to forgive. Understanding human

---

15 This idea is evident in Wesley's understanding of "faith and good works." God's grace and human activity work together, since "God's grace calls forth human responses and discipline. . . . Faith and good works belong within an all-encompassing theology of grace, since they stem from God's gracious love 'shed abroad in our hearts by the Holy Spirit.'" *Book of Discipline 2016,* ¶102, 53.

suffering is a prerequisite for a people-centered church in a global context.

Elisabeth Schüssler Fiorenza, feminist New Testament theologian at Harvard Divinity School, lays out what it means to be a church that embodies the concept of "discipleship of equals." For her, *discipleship* means the practice of "equality from below" in solidarity with all those who struggle for survival and justice.[16] Her understanding of discipleship does not have anything to do with numerical growth; rather it is about equality, freedom, and responsibility, as well as about communal relations free of prejudices and discrimination. For Schüssler Fiorenza, the church needs to be an egalitarian democratic space where the experiences of all people are respected.

> **We can encounter "holiness in life" as we suffer together with wounded people.**

The church is called to respond to the needy, the suffering, and the oppressed. The church is fundamentally social and communal, even as it is expressed and evidenced by individuals. Therefore, it must include people who have been excluded from participating in making decisions for society and make sure that they have opportunity to make decisions in the church.

Christians find meaning and purpose for their *han* in the context of Christ's suffering, and as a result *han* can become a channel of transformation and hope in their lives. The church needs to proclaim that people do not have to be powerless

---

16 Elisabeth Schüssler Fiorenza, *Discipleship of Equals: A Critical Feminist Ekklesia-logy of Liberation* (New York: Crossroad, 1993).

sufferers anymore through the liberating message of Jesus Christ. The transforming power of *han* is evident in the resurrection of Jesus Christ. When the church become a *han-puri madang,* a space where God liberates people through hopeful messages of Jesus Christ, Christians become stronger, resilient, and courageous, boldly speaking and standing up for justice.

Questions for Discussion

1. Why are you a part of the church? What does your church mean to you? What part do you play in making decisions at your church? Who are the leaders in your church?

2. How can your church better serve the congregation? What needs of people do you see that are not fully addressed in your faith community?

3. Share an experience of seeing another person as "other." Share a time when you or someone you know was unfairly excluded. How is God "Other" from us? What would it take for you to connect with the otherness of different people?

4. Think about *han* in your life or in the lives of people who are part of your faith community. How can you and your church help them experience the liberating power of Jesus Christ?

5. Is your church a safe place where people can share their deep sorrow and pain? What has to happen in your church for it to be a *han-puri madang*? What is one thing you can do to make that happen?

4

Creating Vital Cross-Racial and Cross-Cultural Congregations
Preaching, Worship, Music, and Liturgy

This chapter discusses how preaching is a key element for cross-racial and cross-cultural leadership and how it can help create a vital congregation, especially in a multiracial and multicultural setting.

According to research conducted by the General Board of Higher Education and Ministry in 2014, the first and second most important qualities for effective cross-racial and cross-cultural ministry are deep spiritual strength and the clear sense of call and commitment to ministry.[1] A pastor with a deep spiritual strength and a clear sense of call and commitment to ministry has the best chance to prepare and preach sermons that transform and create a vital congregation. With respect to the need of spirituality in the church, 15.8 percent of racial-ethnic pastors consider that meeting the spiritual needs of the church is the most important task for their leadership.[2] Therefore, pastors in a cross-racial

---

1   Park, "Leadership Style of UMC Racial-Ethnic Lead Pastors Who Are Serving Cross-Racial and Cross-Cultural Appointments," 12 (see chap. 2, n. 14).

2   Park, 2.

and cross-cultural setting who are deeply spiritual or who continue practicing spiritual discipline can create a vital congregation with preaching that is sound, biblically grounded, theologically Wesleyan, and applicable or relevant to people's daily lives.

How does a pastor in this context begin to prepare a sermon? A UM CR-CC pastor should prepare and proclaim a sermon with the four living cores of Christian faith: Scripture, tradition, reason, and experience, also called the Wesleyan Quadrilateral.

Scripture

A CR-CC pastor who wants to transform and create a vital congregation should preach the gospel of Jesus Christ with the following essentials of Christian faith either implicitly or explicitly.

First, Jesus Christ is the living Word of God. The Gospel of John proclaims that the Word became flesh (1:14), the Word who "was with God" and "was God," and who participated in the creation of "all things" (1:1-3):

> In the beginning was the Word, and the Word was with God, and the Word was God. He was in the beginning with God. All things came into being through him, and without him not one thing came into being. What has come into being in him was life, and the life was the light of all people. The light shines in the darkness and the darkness did not overcome it. (John 1:1-5)

Second, Jesus is about God's work of salvation. "For God so loved the world that he gave his only Son, so that everyone who believes in him may not perish but may have eternal life. Indeed, God did not send the Son into the world to condemn the world, but in order that the world might be saved through him" (John 3:16-17). This is the heart of the good news for the Fourth Evangelist, that in Jesus, the incarnate Word, the Son of God, one can see and know God in a manner never before possible.

Third, Jesus identifies himself as the only way to God. "I am the way, and the truth, and the life. No one comes to the Father except through me" (John 14:6). The combination of the way and the truth presents both a Christological and an eschatological orientation, which Jesus demonstrated throughout his life and ministry. To recognize Jesus as the truth is to affirm that, as the Word made flesh, Jesus makes the truth of God available to the world (John 1:14, 17-18). When Jesus identifies himself as "the life," he is recalling his self-revelation that is at the heart of the Lazarus narrative. John 11:25 claims God's life-giving powers for Jesus and so serves as the key eschatological announcement of the gospel. Jesus is life because Jesus brings God's gift of life to the world (John 3:15-16). Jesus is the way because he is the access point to God's promise of life.

Fourth, the words of Revelation, with apocalyptic spiritual imagery, beckon us to suspend our pragmatism and enter into its world.[3]

---

3   Christopher C. Rowland, "The Book of Revelation: Introduction, Commentary, and Reflections," in *The New Interpreter's Bible Volume 12* (Nashville: Abingdon Press, 1998), 805-7. Rowland explains *apocalypse*: "that means being prepared to see things from another, unusual, point of view and being open to the possibility that difference of perspective will enrich our view and lead to difference of insight."

Then I saw a new heaven and a new earth; for the first heaven and the first earth had passed away, and the sea was no more. And I saw the holy city, the new Jerusalem, coming down out of heaven from God, prepared as a bride adorned for her husband. And I heard a loud voice from the throne saying, "See, the home of God is among mortals. He will dwell with them; they will be his peoples, and God himself will be with them. He will wipe every tear from their eyes. Death will be no more; mourning and crying and pain will be no more, for the first things have passed away." And the one who was seated on the throne said, "See, I am making all things new." (Rev 21:1-5)

Fifth, Jesus preached good news to the poor; the sick; people of different religious, racial, and ethnic backgrounds; sinners; tax collectors; and women: "The Spirit of the Lord is upon me, because he has anointed me to bring good news to the poor. He has sent me to proclaim release to the captives and recovery of sight to the blind, to let the oppressed go free, to proclaim the year of the Lord's favor" (Luke 4:18-19).

Jesus loved and cared for needy people: "For I was hungry and you gave me food, I was thirsty and you gave me something to drink, I was a stranger and you welcomed me, I was naked and you gave me clothing, I was sick and you took care of me, I was in prison and you visited me. . . . Truly I tell you, just as you did it to one of the least of these who are members of my family, you did it to me" (Matt 25:35-40).

John Wesley also preached good news to the poor and practiced visiting the poor, sick, and imprisoned regularly. As a United Methodist who believes in Jesus and follows John Wesley, a preacher should learn that when we respond to human need, or fail to respond, we are in fact responding or failing to respond to Christ.

Who are "the least of these who are members of my family" in our society?

The book of Revelation contains a repeated pattern of judgment and eschatological resolution. John sees a new heaven and earth replacing the ones that have vanished. The theme of newness of Second Isaiah (Isa 42:9), hinted at in promises to the angels of the seven churches (Rev 2:17; 3:12) and in the song that greets the Lamb, is now fulfilled.

> Jesus loved and cared for needy people.

Through Scripture, the living Christ meets us in the experience of redeeming grace. We are convinced that Jesus Christ is the living Word of God in our midst, whom we trust in life and death. The Bible bears authentic testimony to God's self-disclosure in the life, death, and resurrection of Jesus Christ as well as in God's work of creation, in the pilgrimage of Israel, and in the Holy Spirit's ongoing activity in human history.[4]

Tradition

A CR-CC pastor who wants to create a vital congregation should know the history of the Methodist movement. Wesleyan tradition had its origin both in the Church of England as well as in various dissenters' movements. In addition to those traditions, a pastor in a cross-racial and cross-cultural setting should introduce his or her local tradition and spirituality, such

---

4 "Scripture," in pt. 3, "Doctrinal Standards and Our Theological Task," *Book of Discipline 2016*, ¶105, 83–84.

as African American, African, Asian, Asian Pacific Islander, Hispanic, Afro-Caribbean, European, and so on.

A local tradition—especially spirituality—needs to be in conversation with other local traditions and with our Wesleyan heritage in the task of creating a vital congregation for today.

"As United Methodists, we pursue our theological task in openness to the richness of both the form and power of tradition," especially as we are "challenged by traditions from around the world that accent dimensions of Christian understanding that grow out of the sufferings and victories of the downtrodden. These traditions help us rediscover the biblical witness to God's commitments to the poor, the disabled, the imprisoned, the oppressed, the outcast. In these persons we encounter the living presence of Jesus Christ."[5]

Experience

A CR-CC pastor in the Wesleyan tradition should remember that both personal and corporate experience means "new life in Christ": "So if anyone is in Christ, there is a new creation: everything old has passed away; see, everything has become new!" (2 Cor 5:17). Therefore Christian experience provides pastor and congregations with a new perspective to see the living truth in Scripture. As our experience interacts with Scripture, we read the Bible in light of the conditions and events that help shape who we are, and, likewise, we interpret our experience in terms of Scripture. For instance, sharing stories of a conversion experience, call to ministry, or a personal practice of prayer through sermons

---

5 "Tradition," in *Book of Discipline 2016*, ¶105, 86.

and small group studies might bring, not only new and different aspects of the church life, but also the creation of a vital congregation. While "some facets of human experience tax our theological understanding," many of God's people "live in terror, hunger, loneliness, and degradation. Everyday experiences of birth and death, of growth and life in the created world, and an awareness of wider social relations also belong to serious theological reflection."[6]

Reason

"Although we recognize that God's revelation and our experience of God's grace continually surpass the scope of human language and reason, we also believe that any disciplined theological work or thought calls for the careful use of reason."[7]

A CR-CC pastor who wants to create a vital congregation should empower the congregation and invite them to read and interpret the living Word of God using reason. Reason is God's gift given to us. A pastor should teach the congregation not to fear but to use reason to discern God's will and eventually live out faithful Christian life in the wilderness of the world.

Make me to know your ways, O LORD; teach me your paths. Lead me in your truth, and teach me, for you are the God of my salvation; for you I wait all day long. (Ps 25:4-5)

---

6 "Experience," in *Book of Discipline 2016*, ¶105, 87.
7 "Reason," in *Book of Discipline 2016*, ¶105, 88.

Awake, my soul! Awake, O harp and lyre! I will awake the dawn. (Ps 57:8)

The Lord GOD has given me the tongue of a teacher, that I may know how to sustain the weary with a word. Morning by morning he wakens—wakens my ear to listen as those who are taught. (Isa 50: 4)

That very night the believers sent Paul and Silas off to Beroea; and when they arrived, they went to the Jewish synagogue. These Jews were more receptive than those in Thessalonica, for they welcomed the message very eagerly and examined the scriptures every day to see whether these things were so. (Acts 17:10-11)

There are two crucial roles of reason: (1) with reason, along with faith, pastors interpret the Bible and prepare sermons that hold the possibility for transformation; (2) and with reason, the pastor makes beliefs and traditions about Christ Jesus relevant in the lives of congregations and communities, in other words, to the human condition.

Every sermon needs to touch people's hearts, souls, minds, and hands. Matthew wrote:

"Teacher, which commandment in the law is the greatest?" [Jesus] said to him, "'You shall love the Lord your God with all your heart, and with all your soul, and with all your mind.' This is the greatest and first commandment. And a second is like it: 'You shall love your neighbor as yourself.' On these two commandments hang all the law and the prophets." (Matt 22:36-40)

Following are several sermons, each with a different purpose, but all were delivered by Jung Sun Oh, a pastor in cross-racial and cross-cultural ministry.

Sample Sermon: A Call to Ecological Conversion[8]

A sermon for transforming and creating a vital congregation needs the urgency of salvation. What is salvation? Restoring a broken relationship through Christ Jesus with God, with others, and with God's creation. The sermon is based on Genesis 1–2; Psalm 24; Romans 8:19, 22–23; and Matthew 10:29.

You and I have a problem. The global environmental crisis is a real and very serious problem.

Let me share the following three illustrations of environmental disaster in recent history with you this morning.

(1) Deepwater Horizon Oil Spill in the Gulf of Mexico

The 2010 Deepwater Horizon oil spill in the Gulf of Mexico has been described as the worst environmental disaster in the United States.[9] It released 4.9 million barrels (210 million US gallons).[10] Both the spill and the cleanup efforts had effects on the environment.

(2) Air Pollution in China

---

8   Jung Sun Oh preached this sermon at Bethany First United Methodist Church in Roslindale, Massachusetts, on Sunday, March 9, 2014.

9   Barack Obama, in Reuters Staff, "Full Text of President Obama's BP Oil Spill Speech," Reuters, June 15, 2010, https://www.reuters.com/article/us-oil-spill-obama-text/full-text-of-president-obamas-bp-oil-spill-speech-idUSTRE65F02C20100616.

10 Wikipedia, s.v. "Deepwater Horizon Oil Spill," accessed February 15, 2018, https://en.wikipedia.org/wiki/Deepwater_Horizon_oil_spill.

Outdoor air pollution contributed to 1.2 million prema-ture deaths in China in 2010, nearly 40 percent of the global total, according to a new summary of data from a scientific study on leading causes of death worldwide.[11] *China burns 3.8 billion tons of coal each year, nearly as much as the rest of the world combined.*[12] *"Severe pollution has slashed an aver-age of five and [a] half years from life expectancy in northern China, as toxic air has led to higher rates of stroke, heart dis-ease and cancer."*[13]

(3) Chemical Spill Fouls Water in West Virginia

More than one hundred thousand customers were with-out safe tap water after a chemical used to clean coal leaked into the Elk River in Charleston, West Virginia. "West Virginia American Water warned residents in nine Charleston-area counties not to use the water. Gov. Earl Ray Tomblin declared a state of emergency, urging people not to drink, bathe, cook or wash clothes in the water."[14]

---

11 Edward Wong, "Air Pollution Linked to 1.2 Million Premature Deaths in China," the *New York Times*, April 1, 2013, http://www.nytimes.com/2013/04/02/world/asia/air-pollution-linked-to-1-2-million-deaths-in-china.html.

12 Brad Plume, "China Now Burning as Much Coal as the Rest of the World Combined," the *Washington Post Wonkblog*, Janu-ary 29, 2013, https://www.washingtonpost.com/news/wonk/wp/2013/01/29/china-is-burning-nearly-as-much-coal-as-the-rest-of-the-world-combined/?utm_term=.105bba6bc4d6.

13 Charles Riley, "Air Pollution Cuts Life Expectancy by 5.5 Years in China—Study," CNN Money, July 9, 2013, http://money.cnn.com/2013/07/09/news/china-air-pollution/index.html.

14 Ashley Southall, "Chemical Spill Fouls Water in West Virginia," the *New York Times*, January 9, 2014, https://www.nytimes.com/2014/01/10/us/chemical-spill-fouls-water-in-w-virginia.html.

It is indeed one of the great tragedies of our era that the church, the community of faith, has not focused on developing a biblical, ecological theology. Too often our theologians, pastors, Christian educators, and laity have been silent as our rivers and streams are polluted by industrial wastes; as our air becomes contaminated by poisons that threaten life; as the ozone layer is pierced, exposing human life to deadly radiation; and the food supply is contaminated and the environmental balance is upset by the destruction of the rain forest, trees, and vegetation.

Today's sermon title, "A Call to Ecological Conversion" prompts me to share this biblical interpretation of the texts and theological reflection.

When Christian believers reread Bible passages with the lens of ecological awareness, Christian believers can experience ecological conversion.

I strongly believe that the Judeo-Christian tradition has an important contribution to reversing the current ecological and environmental crisis.

I would like to think about the solutions to respond urgently, creatively, and biblically to the ecological crisis we have created. This is our goal for today.

The Christian faith, especially in the living memory of Jesus as God-with-us bringing healing and liberation, is deeply connected to creation.

Christian believers find ultimate meaning in the idea that God is with us in Jesus of Nazareth and in the grace of the Holy Spirit. This means that the fundamental task of a Christian ecological theology is to show the inner relationship between faith in Jesus of Nazareth and ecological living or commitment.

While we lament the fact that humanity has failed God in its abuse of the planet, God's creation, we can celebrate the beginning of ecological conversion and living and action.

In this movement, Christians are called to humbly take our stance alongside others, many of whom have long led the way in ecological conviction and practice.

What, then, is the task of the church in this movement of conversion? It is called to witness to the God of Jesus Christ, and to God's love for all Earth's creatures. In this process, the church herself is called to ecological conversion.

I acknowledge humbly that there are many instances where Christian tradition has been expressed, interpreted, and lived in an exclusively human-centered (anthropocentric) way, not a God-centered (theocentric) way. I believe rereading texts with an ecological lens leads us to ecological conversion from a human-centered way to a God-centered way.

I would introduce five key themes that can move us beyond a shallow theology of the past toward a deeper level of spiritual awareness and theological insight regarding God's creation and the responsibility of human beings. These key themes are rooted in the Old and New Testament, the spirituality of Francis of Assisi, and the teaching of Dr. Martin Luther King Jr.

Genesis 1 and 2 contain two creation narratives in very different modes, which articulate that the world (heaven and earth) belongs to God, is formed and willed by God, is blessed by God with abundance, and is to be cared for by the human creatures who are deeply empowered but also seriously restrained by God. The creation narratives are an affirmation of the goodness of the world intended by God.[15]

In the opening chapter of Genesis, God is presented as delighting in the diversity of creatures and declaring them all to be good; the light, the seas, the dry land, seed-bearing plants, fruit trees, sun and moon, sea creatures and birds,

---

15 Walter Brueggemann, *An Introduction to the Old Testament: The Canon and Christian Imagination* (Louisville: Westminster John Knox Press, 2003), 31–32.

cattle, creeping things, and wild animals of every kind. All the abundance of and fruitfulness of creation comes from God, who blesses all creatures and says, "Be fruitful and multiply and fill the waters in the seas, and let birds multiply on the earth" (Gen 1:22). The exuberance of life springs from the blessing of the Creator. At the end of the sixth day, after the creation of humans in the image of God and the declaration of their dominion over the other creatures, we are told, "God saw everything that he had made, and indeed, it was very good" (Gen 1:31).

In the second chapter of Genesis, the newly created human being is told to "till" and "keep" what God has given (Gen 2:15). Later, after the flood, the Creator enters into an eternal covenant with Noah that embraces every living creature (Gen 9:12–16). The rainbow is to be the enduring sign of this covenant with all living things. And in the Psalms, God is seen as the one who sustains and nourishes all living things: "You make springs gush forth in the valleys; they flow between the hills, giving drink to every wild animal" (Ps 104:10–11). It is God who gives the breath of life to every creature: "When you send forth your spirit, they are created; and you renew the face of the ground" (Ps 104:30).

When we reread Genesis chapters 1 and 2 with an ecological lens, we realize and learn that God creates each creature, sustains its existence, delights in its goodness, and blesses it with abundance. Human beings are a part of God's creation, interconnected and interrelated with all other creatures, yet called to act responsively before God the Creator within creation.

In these texts and in many others, the Bible sees all creatures in relationship with God. It offers a fundamentally God-centered (theocentric) vision of reality rather than a human-centered (anthropocentric) one.

Some Christians believe that nature is there simply for human beings to exploit. They see human beings as having the right to dominate creation and to use it for their own benefit, without limits or constraints. The result is accelerated global ecological (and climate) change and crisis; pollution of land, seas, and air; and the tragic loss of biodiversity.

The danger of interpreting and justifying human dominion and exploitation of creation is that it takes texts out of context and uses them for this purpose. The command of Genesis to "have dominion" over other creatures comes from an ancient context where nature was seen as alien and terrifying to ordinary, humble, relatively defenseless human beings. It comes from an ancient context when, in the creation narratives of peoples who were neighbors of Israel, human beings were born to be slaves of the gods.

By contrast, Genesis points to the human vocation as a "kingly" one of bringing human intelligence, courage, and work to bear on the land so that herds might flourish and crops might grow.

In the Christian community, Jesus' life and death stand as a radical critique of all dominating views of power and authority (Mark 10:42–45). It is unfaithful to the wider biblical tradition to interpret the "dominion" text as supporting today's ruthless exploitation and the domination of nature by large corporations in our day.

In our own time, many biblical scholars have rejected the traditional interpretation of dominion theology, stressing that we have greatly misunderstood and often distorted this biblical idea and teaching. I believe it must be rejected in an ecological theology of human beings in relation to other creatures. It is the time to put aside such shallow and unbiblical theology since it does not respect the biblical heritage of the goodness of creation, the community of all creatures before

God, the call to humans to act as images of God, or the divine command to cultivate and care for creation (Gen 2:15).

The World Council of Churches and many other Christian churches have rejected as false the idea that human beings have unlimited rights to exploit or damage the natural world. According to Christian social teaching, human beings have moral duties toward the natural world. They do not have absolute powers or rights over nature.

In a God-centered perspective, other forms of life have their own God-given value, intrinsic value that human beings are called to respect.

Romans 8 says, "For the creation waits with eager longing for the revealing of the children of God; for the creation was subjected to futility, not of its own will but by the will of the one who subjected it, in hope that the creation itself will be set free from its bondage to decay and will obtain the freedom of the glory of the children of God. We know that the whole creation has been groaning in labor pains until now" (vv. 19-22).

In the cross of Jesus, Christians find a God who enters into the pain of the world, who suffers with suffering creation. In the resurrection Christian believers find a promise and hope that death does not have the last word.

The Christ event points to a God who not only feels with suffering creation, but who is already at work transforming suffering into life. Our God is a God of boundless and overwhelming love and compassion. God reaches out to every human being and to every sparrow that falls to the ground (Matt 10:29).

Christian believers should proclaim this gospel boldly and present the hope of Jesus Christ to a world caught in a deepening environmental and ecological crisis.

This model of human beings as kin to other creatures within a community of creation is based on the biblical notion *that there is one God, who continually creates all the diverse things that exist, delighting in their goodness (Gen 1:31) and embracing them in covenant life (Gen 9:12–16).*

We find this idea in the spirituality of Francis of Assisi, the patron saint of ecology, and in the theological tradition that is associated with him. Francis of Assisi saw God's creatures as interconnected in one family of creation. He sang, in his Canticle, of other creatures as sisters and brothers to us.[16] This canticle is not simply an expression of naïve piety, but a deliberate attempt by Francis to communicate a kinship approach to creation at a popular level.

Canticle of Brother Sun and Sister Moon of St. Francis of Assisi

Most High, all powerful, all-good Lord! All praise is Yours,
   all glory, all honor, and all blessing.

To You, alone, Most High, do they belong. No mortal lips
   are worthy to pronounce Your Name.

Be praised, my Lord, through all Your creatures, especially
   through my lord Brother Sun,
Who brings the day; and You give light through him
And he is beautiful and radiant in all his splendor!
Of You, Most High, he bears the likeness.

Be praised, my Lord, through Sister Moon and the stars;
In the heavens You have made them bright, precious and
   beautiful.

Be praised, my Lord, through Brothers Wind and Air, and
   clouds

---

16 See Roger D. Sorrell, *St. Francis of Assisi and Nature: Tradition and Innovation in Western Attitudes toward the Environment* (Oxford: Oxford University Press, 1988), 114, 124.

and storms, and all the weather, through which You give
Your creatures sustenance.

Be praised, my Lord, through Sister Water;
she is very useful, and humble, and precious, and pure.

Be praised, my Lord, through Brother Fire,
through whom You brighten the night. He is beautiful and
cheerful, and powerful and strong.

Be praised, my Lord, through our sisters and Mother Earth,
who feeds us and rules us, and produces various fruits with
colored flowers and herbs.

Be praised my Lord, through those who forgive for love of
you; through those who endure sickness and trial.

Happy are those who endure in peace, for by You, Most
High, they will be crowned.

Be praised, my Lord, through our sister Bodily Death, from
whose embrace no living person can escape. Woe
to those who die in mortal sin! Happy those she finds
doing Your most holy will. The second death can do no
harm to them.

Praise and bless my Lord, and give thanks, and serve Him.

I strongly believe that there is a connection between ecological crisis and consumer culture or consumerism. The credo of contemporary consumerism screamed at me from the bumper sticker: "I Shop, Therefore I Am."

We are suffering a crisis of values. We simply must stop continually pumping the moral pollution of rampant consumerism into the heads and hearts of the people.

In our consumer culture, things have become far more important than people and creation. Indeed, people themselves have been turned into things to be used and abused in a society where everything and everyone is a commodity to be bought and sold.

There is a biblical proverb that says, "Where there is no vision, the people perish" (Prov 29:18 KJV). Another translation says, "Where there is no prophecy, the people cast off restraint."

Martin Luther King Jr. recognized the intimate connection between our materialism and all our other problems more than a quarter century ago when he wrote in Where Do We Go from Here? that as a nation we must undergo a radical "revolution of values."[17]

Friends! You and I are called to cultivate and take care of creation. Human beings are part of the unfolding of creation. We are intimately linked to the life-forms of our planet, and to the atmosphere, the soil, and the oceans. Our existence is encompassed by the mystery of God revealed in all variety of creatures that surround us. We are part of them and they are part of us. All of us together reflect the limitless God's love that is our origin.

We were made in the image of God and kin to all the wonderfully diverse plants, insects, birds, and animals of our beautiful planet, and we are called to cultivate and care for the earth and all its creatures.

Friends, let's change our lifestyle from consumer culture or consumerism to ecological living, which invites you and me to preserve and protect God's creation. The apostle Paul reminds us, "Do not be conformed to this world, but be transformed by the renewing of your minds, so that you may discern what is the will of God—what is good and acceptable

---

17 Martin Luther King Jr., Where Do We Go from Here: Chaos or Community? (1967; Boston: Beacon Press, 2010), 196–97.

and perfect" (Rom 12:2). You and I are called to cultivate and take care of God's creation. Amen.

***

Bulletin Insert

Projects for Ecological Living

Adapted from John Hart's "Twelve Projects for Creation Care," in *What Are They Saying about Environmental Theology?* (Mahwah, NJ: Paulist Press, 2004), 134–41.

1. *Develop Environmental Inventories.* Undertake structural and landscape inventories to determine if our buildings are energy efficient, if our insulation can be improved, if our heating and cooling systems need repair or replacement, if more trees (which beautify places and cleanse the air) should be planted to provide summer shade and winter shield, and if lawns can be sown with native grasses, which require little or no maintenance (thereby saving water, eliminating lawn chemicals, and reducing gasoline for lawn mowers— all of which save energy resources, money, the environment, and health). Use energy-efficient windows and solar energy techniques and technologies.

2. *Diminish or Eliminate Use of Minerals and Materials Threatening Life and Health.* Diminish the use of gold and other materials whose extraction or refinement harms the earth and the health of people and other creatures.

3. *Develop Restoration Project Good for Jobs, Species, and the Environment.* Environmental restoration projects for salmon, trout, redwoods, and other threatened or endangered animal or plant species

can provide jobs while conserving environmental integrity for the well-being of human beings and other creatures of God.

4. *Recycle for the Environment and for Community Programs.* Recycling campaigns (newspaper, paper, aluminum cans, corrugated cardboard, glass) should be undertaken. Use chlorine-free recycled paper to eliminate the dumping of toxic paper plant effluents into rivers.

5. *Promote Justice for the Poor and Ethnic, Racial Minorities.* Christians and the Christian faith community have a particular responsibility for their neighbors to ensure that all its members receive an equitable share of Earth's goods. The "least" of Jesus' brothers and sisters, those deprived of food, drink, clothing, shelter, adequate medical care, and judicial fairness (Matt 25:31–46) because of their poverty or minority status in the dominant culture should have not only their basic needs but a fair share of reasonable wants satisfied.

6. *Analyze and Alter Unjust Economic Structures.* In the United States, the wealthiest and most powerful nation in the world, there should be no hunger or homelessness or lack of basic health care. Yet, millions of people in the United States experience one or all of these forms of basic deprivation. "Minimum" wages guarantee poverty; minimal or no health benefits exacerbate it. Economic democracy is at least as important as political democracy. The earth's goods should provide for the needs for all, but this provision is impeded by an existing economic structure controlled by and primarily benefiting a few people instead of the vast

majority. A living wage and safe working conditions, adequate housing, and universal health care are missing from our current economic structure.

7. *Reduce and Eliminate Harmful Chemical Inputs.* Reduce or stop using fertilizers, herbicides, and insecticides to enhance landscapes or increase the production of food and fiber. These additives to the natural environment are harmful to people (those who apply them, especially farmers, farmworkers, and hobby farmers, and those who unknowingly consume them), pets, water supplies, and beneficial soil organisms. Support local and regional organic farmers at farmers' markets and purchase locally grown organic produce. Eliminate excessive fried foods and sugar and replace soft drink dispensers with water and juice vending machines.

8. *Evaluate the Link between Population, Consumption, and Environmental Issues.* The current impasse results in people in the Northern Hemisphere continuing to consume more than their just share of Earth's goods and benefits while blaming the Southern Hemisphere for environmental problems; and in people in the Southern Hemisphere (at times fearful, because of poverty and infant mortality resulting from poverty, poor health care, polluted water, and minimal or no water treatment) having more children than their nation can provide for while condemning the Northern Hemisphere for taking and consuming Southern Hemisphere goods and destroying Southern ecologies.

9. *Form Integrated and Active Alliances and Associations.* Faith groups should reach out to environmental

groups for mutual education and joint projects. Environmental organizations would provide expertise about environmental issues and community projects to care for the environment. Church members would offer their consciousness of the commons as God's creation, and their awareness of local employment needs. Both would be committed to restoring and conserving ecologically important areas while promoting economically sustainable communities.

Sample Sermon: You Did It to Me[18]

Text: Matthew 25:31–46; John 12:1–8

I would like to ask you two questions: the first one is easy and the second one is not easy. First, what is the name of our church? Yes! Bethany! Second, do you know the meaning of the word Bethany? Poor house or House of Misery! According to the gospel passage today, Jesus went to Bethany to spend time with his friends. Biblical village Bethany in Jesus' time! Bethany First UMC in Roslindale in 2013!

Please continue to think using your spiritual imagination about the connection between these two. We are God's children and the people of Bethany First UMC. As you are pondering, I would like to share with you a story this morning. Bethany First celebrated pre-Christmas with children and youth at Washington Beech Street Public Housing in Roslindale on December 15, 2012. It was the last outreach ministry and mission of the Bethany First UMC in 2012.

As you know, Bethany First Church has carried on an outreach ministry and mission in our community since 2006, and it has become the Bethany church tradition. We Bethany

18 Wilbur C. Zigler Preaching Award Sermon 2013, New England Conference of The United Methodist Church.

people go out into the community to share God's love. Bethany celebrates Easter and Christmas with residents in the Washington Beech Street Housing before we celebrate Easter and Christmas at our own church building.

On December 15, the outreach ministry team and other church members joined the pre-Christmas celebration ministry and prayed and distributed Christmas gifts to children and youth. We played games and sang Christmas carols. It was a joyous and blessed Christmas party. In the middle of the party, one of our church participants approached and said to me: "Pastor, you told me that the residents of this public housing are poor and need our support, love, and prayers. I have difficulty understanding what you mean. They are not poor people. They are living in a decent, nice building. Look at this room [fellowship hall] and the building. This building is a new and beautiful apartment complex and condominium and much, much better than my own house."

I told her that "the residents here are the lowest-income people in Boston. Most of them are first-generation immigrants and do not speak English. They depend on the assistance of the federal and state and the city of Boston government. And they do not own these apartments and pay rent. They are the poorest people in our community." And I added, "This apartment and community are their homes, and they need our love and support."

Bethany First will continue to do outreach ministry and mission for our sisters and brothers in our community. We will support and love especially the poor people in our church and in our community. According to the Gospel of John, Bethany was a place where Jesus felt safe, a place he could call home on earth.

Not Bethlehem, where he was born. Not Nazareth, where he grew up. Not Jerusalem, where he preached, taught, and healed people and died.

According to the Gospel of John, before entering into Jerusalem and the final days of his ministry and mission on earth, Jesus visited his favorite place: Bethany. Why was Bethany the favorite place on earth for Jesus?[19]

First of all, Jesus loved and cared for the needy, especially the poor and sick people. Many New Testament scholars tell us that ancient Bethany was the site of an almshouse for the poor and a place of care for the sick.

Lazarus and his two sisters, Mary and Martha, invited Jesus to dinner at their home at Bethany. Martha served. Mary came in with a jar of very expensive aromatic oils and anointed and massaged Jesus' feet. She wiped them with her hair. The fragrance of the oils filled the house. Judas said, "Why wasn't this oil sold and the money given to the poor?" Jesus knew that Judas said this not because he cared for poor people but because he was a thief.

In response to Judas, Jesus said, "Let her alone. She is anticipating and honoring the day of my burial. You always have the poor with you. You don't always have me." Before going further, I would like to note here that some people misunderstand Jesus' response to Judas, that "you will always have the poor with you." Have you ever heard that quote used as a way of saying that there is nothing you can do about poverty?

Some even act as if Jesus meant there is no use in trying to help poor people because you will always have the poor among us. Here Jesus was quoting from Deuteronomy 15, and everyone present knew it. In that chapter, Moses speaks to the people who are on the verge of crossing over to the promised land. Moses tells them that even in a land overflowing with milk and honey there will be poor among them. But

---

19 I am indebted for this idea to Frank Viola, *God's Favorite Place on Earth* (Colorado Springs: David C. Cook, 2013).

Moses goes on to say that it is their responsibility to care for poor people!
  It's not an option!
  It's not charity!
  It is a divine command!
  It is clear that Jesus was saying Christians will always be with the poor, because that is who they are: people who work and live with the poor.

If you were poor in biblical times, you could not maintain your inherited position in the rigid social system of that time. Being poor usually had something to do with money, but it also meant you had been the victim of bad luck (an illness or accident) or of someone else's unfair treatment. To be poor meant your position in your entire community was at risk, including in your family, religious community, employment, and local polities. For example, widows lost their position in the local community completely when their husbands died, so they were always poor no matter how much money they had.

Also, in New Testament times, everything was thought to be in limited quantity. Some were able to accumulate more than others, but only if they had enough power to take it away from the more vulnerable. If you were rich in biblical times, you were either powerful or related to someone in power. It was rare to be rich and honorable. There was no middle class. Everyone was poor, except for the very, very few rich people.[20]

Jesus was telling the busybodies who were worried about what Mary of Bethany was doing not only to mind their own business but to mind to their business—their business of

---

20 See Lallie B. Lloyd, *Eradicating Global Poverty: A Christian Study Guide on the Millennium Development Goals* (New York: National Council of the Churches of Christ in the USA, 2006), 19. Also, Bruce J. Malina and Richard L. Rohrbaugh, *Social Science Commentary on the Synoptic Gospels* (Minneapolis: Fortress Press, 2003), 400-401.

caring for poor people themselves. And we inherit that com-
mand from Jesus.

Rather than criticize others for their giving (I believe Jesus
was certainly pleased by Mary's choice to serve him directly),
we need to constantly refocus our hearts upon our giving to
the work of the gospel.

There is a lot we ought to be doing—and as Jesus and
Moses made clear, it's not optional! It is the Law! A holy Law!

Throughout Israel's history and in early Christianity, the
poor are agents of God's transforming power. "The Spirit of
the Lord is upon me, because he has anointed me to bring
good news to the poor" (Luke 4:18). This was Jesus' first
proclamation.

In the Last Judgment, so dramatically described in the
Gospel of Matthew, we are told that we will be judged accord-
ing to how we respond to the hungry, the thirsty, the stranger,
the naked, and the prisoner (Matt 25:31-46).

As followers of Jesus, we are challenged to make a fun-
damental "option for the poor"—to speak for the voiceless, to
defend the defenseless, to assess styles, policies, and social
institutions in terms of their impact on the poor. This "option
for the poor" does not mean pitting one group against
another, but rather, strengthening the whole community by
assisting those who are most vulnerable.

As Christians, we are called to respond to the needs of
all our brothers and sisters; however, those with the greatest
needs require the greatest response.

More than eight hundred million people suffer from
chronic hunger, and over ten million children die each year
from preventable causes.[21] These may seem like overwhelm-
ing statistics, but as author Stephen C. Smith shows in his call

---

21 Stephen C. Smith, *Ending Global Poverty: A Guide to What Works*
(New York: St. Martin's Griffin, 2005).

to arms, global poverty is something that we can and should solve within our lifetimes.

Jesus found friendship, love, and caring at Bethany. This small settlement was the home of his great friends Lazarus, Martha, and Mary. Jesus wept over Lazarus before calling him forth from his tomb. Now he takes time to celebrate a joyful, special meal with his restored friend. The one who had been laid in his tomb was now reclining at the table alongside Jesus.

Just 1.5 miles outside of Jerusalem, Bethany was still "far enough away." Jesus' best friends—Lazarus, Martha, Mary— kept their home open for him and for his disciples, always welcoming and always open-armed. Yes! Bethany was not where Jesus went to preach or teach. Bethany was where Jesus went to hang out with his "buddies." Martha, Mary, and Lazarus were Jesus' friends. Bethany was a place where Jesus, physically, emotionally, and spiritually, found the strength and support to continue to do his ministry and carry out the mission on earth.

We know that the hometown people of Nazareth threatened Jesus. But no one threatened Jesus at Bethany. Rather, Martha, Mary, and Lazarus welcomed him and shared their genuine love with him. Jesus enjoyed friendship along with good, family-style food at Bethany. Mary's gift of the perfume added another layer to the celebration of that evening.

We know that when Jesus wanted to be alone to pray and communicate with God, he went into the wilderness. Jesus prayed in the wilderness, where he found communion with the God he proclaimed. The Gospels recount Jesus' going out into the wilderness for forty days at the beginning of his ministry. During his ministry Jesus regularly went into the wilderness to find God. Mark describes Jesus getting up early in the morning and going out to a deserted place to pray (Mark 1:35). Luke says that in one of his references to Jesus at prayer, Jesus goes out to a mountain and spends the night in prayer (Luke 6:12)

As Jesus' passion approaches, the Gospels tell of his praying outdoors in the Garden of Gethsemane, where he struggles in darkness and pain and entrusts his life and death to God.

However, when Jesus needed friendship, love, caring, encouragement, and nurturing, he went to Bethany.

Jesus had one special place: Bethany. When Jesus needed fellowship with his closest friends, he traveled to Bethany. Author Frank Viola calls Bethany "Jesus's favorite place on Earth."

It was the place where he felt safe. It was the place where he felt loved. It was the place where he had a close connection to friends who were not evaluating his ministry or criticizing his ministry.

It was the place where Jesus shared his joys, sorrows, concerns, disappointments, and frustrations.

It was the place where Jesus was accepted for who he was.

Jesus' close friendship with women—Mary and Martha of Bethany—was most unusual. He relied on a woman's witness to tell the disciples of the resurrection, giving voice and credibility to a woman when her testimony would not be valid in a court of law.

Jesus gave women dignity and status equal to that of the men in his culture. He healed a woman whose flow of blood made her ritually unclean (Matt 9:20-22; Mark 5:25-29; Luke 8:43-44). He responded to women's pleas on behalf of their children. Many of his most powerful acts of healing were in the context of his relationships with women.[22]

---

22 See Lloyd, *Eradicating Global Poverty*, 31; Malina and Rohrbaugh, *Social Science Commentary on the Synoptic Gospels*, 424-25.

A woman's position in the families of biblical times depended entirely on her relationship to the men in the household. She was a worry to her father because her behavior could cast the whole family into shame, dislodging them permanently from their status and influence in the local community, which was their entire world. Her marriage was rarely, if ever, under her control. It was a legally binding contract negotiated by her extended family that moved her from her father's house to her husband's, where she was considered a stranger until she secured a position of honor by giving birth to a son. Like everyone else in her time, she was emotionally, psychologically, socially, economically, and religiously dependent on her family, which always centered on the male head of the household.

Friends! Do you have a place where you feel safe? A place you can call home, your spiritual home? A place you can be you? Do you have a place where you can be healed, physically, emotionally, and spiritually? I hope and pray that Bethany First UMC, and your church, and every church in the New England Conference, and every church in the global village will be that place and community for you.

Let's remember the needy people and poor people among us at our church and in our community. Let's open our hearts and share God's love with residents of the Washington Beech Street Public Housing, the homeless people of the House of Hope, the lonely and needy people at the Roslindale House, and the needy people who are coming to the Greater Boston Food Bank.

I hope and pray that when you worship and have fellowship at our church, each one of you individually and as a community of faith, you and I hear God's voice saying, "I have called you by name and I love you."

I also hope and pray that when we go out to the community and share God's love with people, especially poor people, you and I hear God's voice saying "Come, you that are blessed by my Father, inherit the kingdom prepared for you from the foundation of the world" (Matt 25:34).

We go outside four walls and into a community and share God's love with poor and needy people.

We are God's children and people of the New England Conference. Let us pray with the poem that is attributed to Teresa of Ávila (1515–82),[23] a sixteenth-century mystic: "Christ has no body now on earth but yours, no hand but yours no feet but yours. Yours are the eyes through which to look out Christ's compassion to the world; yours are the feet with which he is to go about doing good; yours are the hands with which he is to bless men now."

Friends! Let's remember the saying of Jesus Christ, "Truly I tell you, just as you did it to one of the least of these who are members of my family, you did it to me" (Matt 25:40). Let's go to the streets in our neighborhoods and serve God's people who are hungry, thirsty, stranger, naked, sick, and in prison. Let's share God's love with God's people who are desperately in need of our prayers, compassion, and love. Amen.

Preaching in Cross-Racial and Cross-Cultural Congregations

As mentioned earlier, preaching is one of the most crucial elements for creating a vital congregation. Therefore a preacher in cross-racial and cross-cultural ministry should prepare a sermon that is biblically grounded, theologically

---

23 Born in Spain, Teresa entered a Carmelite convent when she was eighteen and later earned a reputation as a mystic, reformer, and writer who experienced divine visions. She founded a convent and wrote the book *The Way of Perfection* for her nuns. Other important books by her include her *Autobiography* and *The Interior Castle*.

Wesleyan, and applicable or relevant to the daily lives of the congregation. A pastor should prepare his or her sermon with daily Bible reading and exegesis, meditation, prayer, and theological reflection on events that are affecting the lives of the congregation and communities in local and global situations.

According to recent research covering racial-ethnic clergy who are serving large Caucasian-majority churches, the foremost quality for effective cross-cultural and cross-racial ministry is deep spiritual strength and a clear sense of call and commitment to ministry. Racial-ethnic lead pastors who are serving large Caucasian-majority churches spend significantly more time preparing for preaching, with 21.6 percent of them spending sixteen to twenty hours on sermon preparation, while 8.9 percent of white lead pastors spend the same amount of time.[24]

They also agree that meeting the spiritual needs of the church is the most important task for their leadership. A pastor who has deep spiritual strength and a clear sense of call and commitment to ministry can prepare and preach a sermon that creates a vital congregation.

As Marjorie Thompson points out poignantly, we are living in a time of deepest thirst and spiritual hunger.

> There is a hunger abroad in our time, haunting lives and hearts. Like an empty stomach aching beneath the sleek coat of a seemingly well-fed creature, it reveals that something is missing from our largely rational, secular, and affluent culture. If we look at the

---

24 Park, "Leadership Style of UMC Racial-Ethnic Lead Pastors Who Are Serving Cross-Racial and Cross-Cultural Appointments," 10–12 (see chap. 2, n. 14).

underbelly of this sleek creature, we notice ragged, unkempt fur and signs of disease. Even in communities that hold sacred values, much is awry. Both within and beyond traditional faith communities, a hunger for spiritual depth and integrity has been gaining momentum for several generations.[25]

While sociologists may attribute the universal human religious impulse to psychosocial need, people of faith believe that we are made for relationship with God. Therefore until that relationship is sought and found, there will always be an existential emptiness at the core of our being or becoming. Centuries ago, Saint Augustine confessed to God, "You have made us for yourself, and our heart is restless until it rests in you."[26]

Both the Old and New Testaments illustrate the deepest spiritual hunger of human beings. The psalmist expressed the longing for God poetically, "As a deer longs for flowing streams, so my soul longs for you, O God. My soul thirsts for God, for the living God. When shall I come and behold the face of God?" (Ps 42:1-2).

> Something is missing from our largely rational, secular, and affluent culture.

Our spiritual hunger is evidence of the timeless human need for a real and abiding relationship with God. The Holy One calls us into this relationship and does everything possible to restore us when we have wriggled out of its

---

25 Marjorie J. Thompson, *Soul Feast: An Invitation to the Christian Spiritual Life* (Louisville: Westminster John Knox Press, 2014), 1.

26 Saint Augustine, *Confessions*, trans. Henry Chadwick (New York: Oxford University Press, 1991), 3.

mutual demands. God's love lies at the root of our hunger for God. Indeed, love is God's hunger for relationship with us.

We are like the prodigal son of Jesus' parable in Luke 15:11-32. The prodigal son was far from home and starving. "So he set off and went to his father. But while he was still far off, his father saw him and was filled with compassion; he ran and put his arms around him and kissed him" (v. 20). Like the prodigal son, have we decided to go home?

We remember the dialogue between a Samaritan woman and Jesus in the Gospel of John. "Jesus said to her, 'Everyone who drinks of this water will be thirsty again, but those who drink of the water that I will give them will never be thirsty. The water that I will give will become in them a spring of water gushing up to eternal life'" (John 4:13-14).

Bishops William R. Cannon and William R. Harmon, who served as resident bishops at Emory University Candler School of Theology in the 1980s and 1990s, taught seminary students that a preacher must spend at least twenty hours preparing a Sunday sermon. Preparing a sermon is and should be an ongoing practicing spiritual discipline for a pastor. Spiritual disciplines include lectio divina, journaling, daily prayer, spiritual reading, confession, discussion with a spiritual guide, and simplicity (nature).

The questions arise: How can a preacher spend at least twenty hours for sermon preparation each week? And why? It is only possible when a pastor realizes and practices sermon preparation itself as an ongoing practicing spiritual discipline.

The Bible as Foundation

The Bible is and should be the primary foundation for preaching. The Bible, or Scripture, must be the focus of disciplined study. According to Wesley, the core of Christian faith is (a) revealed in Scripture, (b) illuminated by tradition, (c) made vivid in personal experience, and (d) confirmed by reason.

The following daily schedule shows a practical way to prepare a biblically grounded, theologically sound, and relevant sermon each week.

Monday: Bible reading (and listening with audio portion), exegesis, reflection, and prayer (you might follow the lectionary or choose scriptures based on your sermon topic.) Write down the ideas or themes that occurred.

Tuesday: Bible reading (and listening with audio portion), exegesis, reflection, and prayer. Pay attention to events or crimes or natural disasters that are affecting the lives of the congregation and local community. Then begin theological reflection on those events or crimes or natural disasters.

Wednesday: Bible reading (and listening with audio portion), reflection, and prayer. Pay attention to events or wars or natural disasters that are affecting the lives of God's people in the global village. Then start theological reflection on those events or wars or natural disasters.

Thursday: Bible reading (and listening with audio portion), reflection, and prayer. Start writing the first draft of the sermon.

Friday: Bible reading (and listening with audio portion), reflection, and prayer. Finish the manuscript of the sermon. Start to memorize the sermon.

Saturday: Bible reading (and listening with audio portion), prayer. Memorize the whole sermon.

Sunday: Preach the sermon.

Worship in Cross-Racial and Cross-Cultural Congregations

God is Spirit, and those who worship him must worship in spirit and truth. (John 4:24)

As a deer longs for flowing streams, so my soul longs for you, O God. My soul thirsts for God, for the living God. When shall I come and behold the face of God? (Ps 42:1-2)

Praise the LORD!
Praise God in his sanctuary;
   praise him in his mighty firmament!
Praise him for his mighty deeds;
   praise him according to his surpassing greatness!

Praise him with trumpet sound;
   praise him with lute and harp!
Praise him with tambourine and dance;
   praise him with strings and pipe!
Praise him with clanging cymbals;
   praise him with loud clashing cymbals!
Let everything that breathes praise the LORD!
Praise the LORD! (Psalm 150)

Worship is where we express love and devotion to God. Why do congregations gather together to worship? People are hungry for love, grace, and the forgiveness of God that comes through worship. Thomas G. Long further explains:

Worshiping God is not simply a good thing to do; it is a necessary thing to do to be human. The most profound statement that can be made about us is that we need to join with others in bowing before God in worshipful acts of devotion, praise, obedience,

103

thanksgiving, and petition. What is more, when all the clutter is cleared away from our lives, we human beings do not merely need to engage in corporate worship; we truly want to worship in communion with others. All of us know somewhere in our hearts that we are not whole without such worship, and we hunger to engage in that practice.[27]

So the next question CR-CC pastors and worship team leaders should ask is, "What are our deepest needs as people of God?" Long responds:

First and foremost, we need mystery, that is, we need God. Specifically, we need to be in communion with God, to belong to God, to be in right and loving relationship with God. The 16th century Heidelberg Cathechism points to this need to belong to God when it begins with the following question and answer: "What is your only comfort, in life and in death? That I belong—body and soul, in life and in death—not to myself but to my faithful Savior, Jesus Christ."[28]

We, as people of God, need each other as well. Long says that "because we belong to God, we need to join ourselves in community with others to give ourselves away to God, to offer our lives to something larger than ourselves, something that provides meaning and lets us know that our lives count for something of ultimate value."[29]

---

27 Thomas G. Long, *Beyond the Worship Wars: Building Vital and Faithful Worship* (Lanham, MD: Alban Institute, 2001), 16–17.
28 Long, 19.
29 Long, 19.

When these two needs are met in worship—mystery as revealed in God, and communal meaning, or vertical direction with a horizontal dimension—worship can provide flowing streams of living water to hungry people.

So, what is the role of CR-CC pastors and worship team leaders? As Thomas G. Long clearly points out, pastors and worship team leaders cannot control or arrange an encounter with God. So what *is* their role? Long explains:

> **Worship is where we express love and devotion to God.**

Now obviously, an encounter with God is not something that human beings control or arrange. No worship planning team could or should sit around a table brainstorming ways for holiness to erupt in the order of worship. However, while we certainly do not have the power to make God appear, a service of worship is a somewhat fragile medium, and we do have, it seems, the negative capacity to create static, to sabotage people's perception of God's presence. God is present in worship; our job is to clear the clutter and get out of the way of people's sight lines.[30]

The purpose of this chapter about worship is (1) to help CR-CC pastors and worship teams understand the nature of worship; (2) to equip CR-CC pastors and worship teams to renew and create worship services that are biblically grounded, theologically sound, and culturally relevant; and (3) to transform lives and create vital congregations.

---

30 Long, 21.

Worship services that are biblically grounded, theologically sound, and culturally relevant should involve the meeting of God's heart and our hearts so that we experience God's presence and the release, redemption, renewal, and restoration that result. God's deepest desire is that we offer our whole hearts in worship so that God might dwell among us.

Biblical Foundation or Principles for Worship

The Scriptures characterize worship using a number of central themes. There are five themes that are significant to a biblical understanding of worship.[31]

1. Worship Is Centered in God's Acts of Salvation

Who initiates worship? The answer is God. We worship God with worshipful acts of devotion, praise, obedience, thanksgiving, and petition.

Cherry presents the exodus as the central saving event in the Old Testament, and the resurrection of Jesus Christ in the New Testament.[32]

Moses and Israel sang this song (the full story is found in Exodus 1-15):

I will sing to the LORD, for he has triumphed gloriously;
horse and rider he has thrown into the sea.
The LORD is my strength and my might,

---

31 The following themes are adapted from Constance M. Cherry, *The Worship Architect: A Blueprint for Designing Culturally Relevant and Biblically Faithful Services* (Grand Rapids: Baker Academic, 2010).
32 Cherry, 5.

and he has become my salvation;
this is my God, and I will praise him,
my father's God, and I will exalt him. (Exod 15:1-2)

The Christ event is the story of Jesus' life, death, resurrection, and ascension in the Gospels. The early Christian community celebrated the salvation of God in Christ, singing:

[Christ Jesus], who though he was in the form of God,
did not regard equality with God
as something to be exploited,
but emptied himself,
taking the form of a slave,
being born in human likeness.
And being found in human form,
he humbled himself
and became obedient to the point of death—
even death on a cross.
Therefore God also highly exalted him
and gave him the name
that is above every name,
so that at the name of Jesus
every knee should bend,
in heaven and on earth and under the earth,
and every tongue should confess
that Jesus Christ is Lord,
to the glory of God the Father. (Phil 2:6-11)

Cherry insists that

the Christ Event now drives worship, for the object of our worship is Jesus Christ, and the content of our worship is the story of Jesus Christ. The Word proclaimed in Christian worship is the gospel of our

Lord and Savior, Jesus Christ, and the sacramental "ratification" of our worship is our active participation at the Lord's Table, the celebration of the victory of our Lord Jesus Christ over sin and death. The spoken word attests to Christ Jesus through proclamation; [while] the Eucharist offers a symbolic re-presentation of the same.[33]

We, as people of God, who experience and celebrate the salvation of God through Christ Jesus, should act and offer a response. This is worship.

As pastors and leaders of a CR-CC congregation, we should consider who the people God has gathered in our congregation are. How are they moved? And how do our congregations receive the act of salvation and offer a response of joy? I (Jung Sun Oh) learned that Afro-Caribbean church members at Bethany First UMC (Roslindale, MA) freely expressed their joy of salvation as they sang hymns, and also as they prayed during Sunday services.

2. Worship Is Patterned in Revelation and Response

God's act of salvation invites human response. "Worship is the response we make to the gifts of God."[34] Cherry says, "God reveals God's heart, and human beings respond with their hearts to God."[35] Cherry describes this in detail:

Christian worship is always a response to truth, the truth as revealed in Jesus Christ. This sequence is

---

33 Cherry, 8.
34 Ralph P. Martin, *Worship in the Early Church* (Grand Rapids: Eerdmans, 1974), 16.
35 Cherry, *The Worship Architect*, 8.

the native pattern of worship: it is the natural result of what happens when humanity encounters God. It forms the basis for the simplest service of Word and Table; the Word is revealed and worshipers respond with Eucharist (thanksgiving). Revelation-response is the normative pattern of dialogue between God and the worshiping community. The reciprocity inherent in a true worship experience is a beautiful thing in which to participate; it is a living, vital conversation, not a religious program.[36]

Pastors and leaders of CR-CC congregations should remember that worshipers in our congregations might have a quite different understanding and experience of revelation/response. In my (Jung Sun Oh) experience as a CR-CC pastor of Bethany First UMC, most church members who regularly attend healing service openly shared with other worshipers that they experienced God's revelation and God's healing with prayers for healing, laying on of hands, and anointing with oil.

3. Worship Is Covenantal in Nature

Worship is the corporate expression and response to the covenantal relationship between God and God's people. Covenant provides identity to the people, the children of God.

The first covenant in the Old Testament is beween God and Noah: "It shall be a sign of the covenant between me and the earth," God said (Gen 9:13). However, the primary Old Testament covenant was that between God and Abram. God promised:

---

36 Cherry, 9.

I will make you exceedingly fruitful; and I will make nations of you, and kings shall come from you. I will establish my covenant between me and you, and your offspring after you throughout their generations, for an everlasting covenant, to be God to you and to your offspring after you. And I will give to you, and to your offspring after you, the land where you are now an alien, all the land of Canaan, for a perpetual holding; and I will be their God. (Gen 17:6-8)

In the New Testament, on the night before his death, Jesus celebrated the Passover meal with his disciples and said, "This cup that is poured out for you is the new covenant in my blood" (Luke 22:20). Cherry explains the relationship between the Lord's Supper and worship:

The sign act of the new covenant is the Table of the Lord, the participation in the bread and the cup as instituted by Jesus and celebrated at least weekly by the early church. It became the culminating act of worship in response to hearing and receiving the word of God. To experience the Eucharist was to experience the covenantal relationship. As Hughes O. Old rightly points out, "Because Christians have shared the Lord's Supper, a covenantal bond has been established and obligates them to Christ alone."[37]

As the early Christians practiced, so we also celebrate the Lord's Supper (Acts 2:42, 46) and pray in the name of Jesus (Acts 4: 24-30) during the worship service.

---

37 Cherry, 11-12, citing Hughes Oliphant Old, *Themes and Variations for a Christian Doxology: Some Thoughts on the Theology of Worship* (Grand Rapids: Eerdmans, 1992), 117.

4. Worship Is Corporate in Nature

Christian worship has always been corporate worship. In his letter to the Christians in Corinth, the apostle Paul described the nature of the corporate church : "For just as the body is one and has many members, and all the members of the body, though many, are one body, so it is with Christ. . . . Indeed, the body does not consist of one member but of many" (1 Cor 12:12, 14).

> Christian worship has always been corporate worship.

Jesus also affirmed the nature of the corporate church: "For where two or three are gathered in my name, I am there among them" (Matt 18:20).

Therefore we worship as the community of faith on Sunday and at other weekly services. We, as people of God, gather together, praise God, pray to God, give thanks to God, hear the Word of God, celebrate the Lord's Supper, and have Christian fellowship.

CR-CC churches, in participating in all of these activities, also reflect in their membership the changing demographics. God is calling pastors and leaders of CR-CC churches of all races, ethnicities, and cultures to proclaim the gospel of Jesus Christ and the coming of God's kingdom, and at the same time, to celebrate diversity and unity in God as revealed through Jesus Christ. These pastors and leaders should realize that the ministry and mission of CR-CC churches embody and rejoice diversities as gifts to the human family. CR-CC churches welcome all people into the community of faith without discrimination because of color, race, ethnicity, language, or culture. Furthermore, CR-CC churches make multiracial and multicultural inclusiveness a key organizing principle for the church in society, for justice and peace throughout the global village or global community.

To be together was a necessary component for experiencing the presence of Christ in New Testament times: "For where two or three are gathered in my name, I am there among them" (Matt 18:20). True public worship cannot happen without a biblical understanding of its corporate nature.

5. Worship Is a Transformational Journey

Luke 24:13-35 is an example of a transformational journey. Jesus and two disciples traveled from Jerusalem to Emmaus on the same road together. Jesus asked the two disciples, "What are you discussing with each other while you walk along?" (v. 17).

One of them responded, "Are you the only stranger in Jerusalem who does not know the things that have taken place there in these days?"

"What things?" he asked them.

They replied, "The things about Jesus of Nazareth, who was a prophet mighty in deed and word before God and all the people, and how our chief priests and leaders handed him over to be condemned to death and crucified him" (vv. 18-20).

Jesus then explained the scripture to them: "'Oh, how foolish you are, and how slow of heart to believe all that the prophets have declared! Was it not necessary that the Messiah should suffer these things and then enter into his glory?' Then beginning with Moses and all the prophets, he interpreted to them the things about himself in all the scriptures" (vv. 25-27).

The two disciples next invited Jesus to dinner and fellowship: "They urged him strongly, saying, 'Stay with us, because it is almost evening and the day is now nearly over.' So he went in to stay with them" (v. 29). When the meal was served, Jesus broke the bread and gave it to the two disciples. Then, we are told, "their eyes were opened, and they recognized him; and he vanished from their sight" (vv. 30–31).

Excited, the two disciples, as witnesses of the risen Lord, "got up and returned to Jerusalem; and they found the eleven and their companions gathered together. They were saying, 'The Lord has risen indeed, and he has appeared to Simon!' Then they told what had happened on the road, and how he had been made known to them in the breaking of the bread" (vv. 33–35).

Cherry summarizes the two disciples' transformational journey from grief and confusion to recognizing the risen Lord as follows:

> There was a transformation in the disciples that took place over time as a result of the whole conversation. Their encounter with Jesus was not a journey simply because they were traveling the same road together. Rather, their encounter was a journey because they progressed spiritually, from their places of origin (grief and confusion), through necessary terrain (explanation of the scripture), and finally to their destination (recognizing the risen Lord).[38]

The apostle Paul connects "the spiritual worship" with transformation and the renewing of our minds, "I appeal to you therefore, brothers and sisters, by the mercies of God, to present your bodies as a living sacrifice, holy and acceptable to God, which is your spiritual worship. Do not be conformed to this world, but be transformed by the renewing of your

---

38 Cherry, 16.

minds, so that you may discern what is the will of God—what is good and acceptable and perfect" (Rom 12:1-2).

Therefore worship is so much more than an emotional, feel-good experience. It is more than a program at local church or a concert by a worship leader. Worship is all about God and God's people. Therefore, worship can transform us.

As contemporary worshipers in a sound-bite world, where interaction can be brief and attention spans short, we do well to remind ourselves that Christian worship is a sustained encounter with God—a journey from our place of origin (physically and spiritually), through meaningful acts of worship as a community, to transformation from having been in God's presence. The journey is the point. Pastors and leaders in CR-CC churches should encourage and remind the congregation that they are on the journey of transformation individually and communally.

In conclusion, true worship has many expressions and attributes, but to sum it up, biblical worship is the effort to be faithful to our best understanding of the ways that God has related to God's covenanted people throughout the Old and New Testaments and to apply these patterns in appropriate ways in our context today.

Studying Your Context

To know who you are, you need to examine where you are and where you have been. Looking at the social and demographic characteristics of the local community sheds light on the people to whom we hope to minister. We may want to consider two parts of a community in context: the local congregation, with its unique traditions, and our immediate community—the neighborhood.

Who are we? Nancy L. Eiesland and R. Stephen Warner introduce the use of an "ecological frame" to analyze the congregation.[39] With ecological framing, the congregation is analyzed as a unit interacting with other units in society: individuals, organizations, and cultures. Eiesland and Warner use a three-layer conceptualization to speak of the social fabric of the community as a complex web of people, meanings, and relationships. They explain the three layers thus:

> The first layer is *demography,* or the characteristics of the people in the community, described in terms of numbers, age, and sex distribution; ethnic and racial profile; and changes in these data over time. The second layer is *culture,* or the systems of meaning, values, and practices shared by (and cognitive of) members of the community and groups within the community. The third layer is *organization,* or the systems of roles and relationships that structure the interactions of people in the community. These three levels help us understand the complex dynamics of the community.[40]

Zac Hicks, canon for worship and liturgy at Cathedral Church of the Advent in Birmingham, Alabama, also insists that to study our community, we should ask:

- What makes my culture tick?
- What kinds of music, movies, and art do they enjoy or find expression in?

---

39 Nancy L. Eiesland and Stephen Warner, "Ecology: Seeing the Congregation in Context," in *Studying Congregations: A New Handbook*, ed. Nancy T. Ammerman et al. (Nashville: Abingdon Press, 1998), 40.
40 Eiesland and Warner, 42.

- How do people in our community express various emotions—joy, fear, hope, longings, lamentation, wonder?
- What are my culture's values, and how are they represented in my town or city's life, layout, architecture, leisure activities?
- What moves people in my city and region?
- What drives decision-making for the people and groups represented in my community?[41]

Carl S. Dudley and Nancy T. Ammerman suggest creating a People Map to help a congregation better understand and make connections with the variety of people who live in our community.[42] On a page they title "Working Notes: Who Shares Our Community?" they ask the following questions:

- From your own personal experience with the community you have identifed what concentrations of people are part of this community?
- Are there language groups?
- Are there distinct religious groups (including people of no faith)?
- Are there different income and social-class groups?
- Are there groups identified by need or lifestyle?
- Are there other important groupings?[43]

---

41 Zac Hicks, *The Worship Pastor: A Call to Ministry for Worship Leaders and Teams* (Grand Rapids: Zondervan, 2016), 106.
42 Carl S. Dudley and Nancy T. Ammerman, *Congregations in Transition: A Guide for Analyzing, Assessing, and Adapting in Changing Communities* (San Francisco: Jossey-Bass, 2002), 29.
43 Dudley and Ammerman, 32.

The answers to these questions will inform you and your congregation of the unique needs of your community and how you can move forward with meeting these needs through ministry.

So, who are we? In connection with worship, we need to ask this question at the historical, the institutional, and the denominational level. We do this by exploring what the worship practices of our local church and of United Methodists have historically been.

Regardless of the theological stances of our churches—evangelical, conservative, progressive—many of us are involved in learning from the tradition of contemporary worship music and practices. The theology and history behind this modern, cross-denominational movement are very much worth studying, appreciating, and understanding, because they are shaping the sensibilities of church members.

And we must remember our cultural context, with its obsession with youth. Sometimes we, as pastors and worship teams, neglect the needs of people from different generations and ignore the biblical wisdom that admonishes us to listen to the Spirit's work among the older generations in our communities (Job 12:12; Prov 7:6-8; 20:29; 1 Tim 5:1-2). Proper contextualization (being a faithful missionary to your flock) involves listening to every voice, not just the young and attractive.

Bringing together considerations of your church and your community often means making some important decisions about worship expressions. Inevitably, some of your church's personal and communal history and practices will stand in tension with what you might employ as you consider the surrounding culture. Pastors and worship team leaders should resolve this tension with prayer and dialogue among our church leadership.

Worship and Culture

Worship is contextual and cross-cultural. When the Calvin Institute of Christian Worship articulated their ten core convictions about worship, one of those convictions was an open and "discerning approach to culture."[44] They said, "Worship should strike a healthy balance among four approaches or dimensions to its cultural context: worship is *transcultural* (some elements of worship are beyond culture), *contextual* (worship reflects the culture in which it is offered), *cross-cultural* (worship breaks barriers of culture through worship), and *counter-cultural* (worship resists the idolatries of its cultural context)."[45]

We find a vision of the contextual and cross-cultural aspects of worship in the book of Revelation:

> I saw no temple in the city, for its temple is the Lord God the Almighty and the Lamb. And the city has no need of sun or moon to shine on it, for the glory of God is its light, and its lamp is the Lamb. The

---

44 Sandra Maria Van Opstal, *The Next Worship: Glorifying God in a Diverse World* (Downers Groves, IL: InterVarsity Press, 2016), 19. A great library of resources on worship can be found at the Calvin Institute's website: http://worship.calvin.edu.

45 Calvin Institute of Christian Worship, "Ten Core Convictions," Calvin.edu, accessed February 16, 2018, https://worship.calvin .edu/resources/resource-library/ten-core-convictions/. These categories (transcultural, cross-cultural, contextual, counter-cultural) are, in turn, adapted from the Nairobi Statement on Worship and Culture, developed by the Lutheran World Federation.

nations will walk by its light, and the kings of the earth will bring their glory into it. Its gates will never be shut by day—and there will be no night there. People will bring into it the glory and the honor of the nations. But nothing unclean will enter it, nor anyone who practices abomination or falsehood, but only those who are written in the Lamb's book of life. (Rev 21:22-27)

In the end the faith community consists of every nation, tribe, people, and language (Rev 7:9). When we worship God, this is a breathtaking picture of God's reign in action.

The apostle Paul, in his letter to the Christians in Rome and Corinth, said that God calls all people to God:

For I am not ashamed of the gospel; it is the power of God for salvation to everyone who has faith, to the Jew first and also to the Greek. For in it the righteousness of God is revealed through faith for faith; as it is written, "The one who is righteous will live by faith." (Rom 1:16-17)

All this is from God, who reconciled us to himself through Christ, and has given us the ministry of reconciliation; that is, in Christ God was reconciling the world to himself, not counting their trespasses against them, and entrusting the message of reconciliation to us. So we are ambassadors for Christ, since God is making his appeal through us; we entreat you on behalf of Christ, be reconciled to God. (2 Cor 5:18-20)

God also calls God's people to one another. Paul wrote to the Ephesians:

For he is our peace; in his flesh he has made both groups into one and has broken down the dividing wall, that is, the hostility between us. He has abolished the law with its commandments and ordinances, that he might create in himself one new humanity in place of the two, thus making peace, and might reconcile both groups to God in one body through the cross, thus putting to death that hostility through it. (Eph 2:14-16)

In worship we celebrate that "in Christ God was reconciling the world to himself" and we practice reconciliation as "ambassadors for Christ." Reconciliation is not something we add to our worship; it is a practice in which we live out our true nature as one new humanity. Reconciliation and worship are interconnected.

Worship is not only contextual but also cross-cultural. It has the potential to connect people's varied narratives. Revelation provides a picture of the kingdom community at the end of time:

After this I looked, and there was a great multitude that no one could count, from every nation, from all tribes and peoples and languages, standing before the throne and before the Lamb, robed in white, with palm branches in their hands. They cried out in a loud voice, saying,

"Salvation belongs to our God who is seated on the throne, and to the Lamb!"

And all the angels stood around the throne and around the elders and the four living creatures, and they fell on their faces before the throne and worshiped God, singing,

"Amen! Blessing and glory and wisdom
and thanksgiving and honor
and power and might
be to our God forever and ever! Amen." (Rev 7:9-12)

Therefore we pray the Lord's Prayer and foretaste God's kingdom here and now.

Our Father in heaven,
    hallowed be your name.
Your kingdom come.
    Your will be done,
    on earth as it is in heaven.
Give us this day our daily bread.
    And forgive us our debts,
as we also have forgiven our debtors.
    And do not bring us to the time of trial
but rescue us from the evil one. (Matt 6:9-13)

Look at the daily news, with its racism, ethnic cleansing, gun violence and massacre, civil unrest, wars, genocide, abuse, gender discrimination, and sexual orientation discrimination. These plague our relationships and hinder cross-cultural engagement. Our faith calls us not only to dream and hope for the day when God's kingdom comes, but Scripture also calls us to be a foretaste of God's kingdom now. We ought not to be influenced by what we see around us; we should instead live into a worship that models something distinct from the rest of the world.

The apostle Paul, in his letter to the Romans, clearly instructed:

I appeal to you therefore, brothers and sisters, by the mercies of God, to present your bodies as a living sacrifice, holy and acceptable to God, which is your spiritual worship. Do not be conformed to this world, but be transformed by the renewing of your minds, so that you may discern what is the will of God—what is good and acceptable and perfect. . . . Let love be genuine; hate what is evil, hold fast to what is good; love one another with mutual affection; outdo one another in showing honor. Do not lag in zeal, be ardent in spirit, serve the Lord. Rejoice in hope, be patient in suffering, persevere in prayer. Contribute to the needs of the saints; extend hospitality to strangers. (Rom 12:1-2; 9-13).

"Biblical community is lived out across many differences," says Sandra Maria Van Opstal: "racial, cultural, ethnic, socioeconomic, [and] theological." The early church itself was a multiethnic, multilingual, global community. Van Opstal further explains:

In the practice of cooperative worship, no matter how different we are, we share in one common narrative in which we remember we are collectively the people of God. Yes, we are many nations. Yes, those differences are significant and beautiful. Yes, they cause natural tensions. In worship, however, we recite, reflect, and remember that God has joined us together to learn from one another how to best glorify God as a corporate body.[46]

46 Van Opstal, *The Next Worship*, 36.

Worship and Justice

Concern for justice is one of the most crucial themes that run through the Old and the New Testaments. The Old Testament prophet Amos connected justice with personal, communal human life, and with the presence of God: "Seek the LORD and live, or he will break out against the house of Joseph like fire, and it will devour Bethel, with no one to quench it. Ah, you that turn justice to wormwood, and bring righteousness to the ground" (Amos 5:6-7). To experience the presence of God, in Amos's view, Israel individually and communally must practice justice, so clearly, worship and justice are linked: "I hate, I despise your festivals, and I take no delight in your solemn assemblies. Even though you offer me your burnt offerings and grain offerings, I will not accept them; and the offerings of well-being of your fatted animals I will not look upon. Take away from me the noise of your songs; I will not listen to the melody of your harps. But let justice roll down like waters, and righteousness like an ever-flowing stream" (Amos 5:21-24). Amos also linked justice with life. Life in the desert requires water. Life in the community requires justice. When Israel does not practice justice, the community withers and its worship rings false.

The Gospel according to Luke provides rich resources on justice. Jesus practiced radical inclusiveness in his ministry and reached out to sinners, tax collectors, the Samaritan, women, and the poor. The gospel calls the Christian community to follow the teachings and footsteps of Jesus Christ, who had concern for the oppressed, the overlooked, and the outcast. God calls us to go beyond our comfort zone to reach out to the poor, the oppressed,

> **Jesus practiced radical inclusiveness in his ministry.**

and the "least of these" among God's people in our community (see Matt 25:31–40). And God reminds pastors and worship team leaders that our acts of justice and mercy are directly connected with worship: "Truly I tell you, just as you did [an act of mercy] to one of the least of these who are members of my family, you did it to me." (Matt 25:40).

Worship connects two dimensions of relationship, our vertical relationship with God and our horizontal relationship with other human beings. As Mark Labberton defines it, "worship is the way human beings are created to reflect God's glory by embodying God's character in lives that seek righteousness and do justice."[47] Labberton insists that not only does worship include "the glory and honor due to God—Father, Son, and Spirit"; it "also includes the enactment of God's love and justice, mercy and kindness in the world."[48] He then explains:

> Worship, then, refers to something very big and very small, and much in between. It can point to the meaning and work of the whole created order. Worship can also be in the cry of a mother or in the joy of a new being or a new disciple. Worship can name a Sunday gathering of God's people, but it also includes how we treat those around us, how we spend our money, and how we care for [the hungry, the thirsty, the stranger, the naked, the sick, the prisoner,] the lost and the oppressed. Worship can encompass every dimension of our lives.[49]

---

47 Mark Labberton, *The Dangerous Act of Worship: Living God's Call to Justice* (Downers Grove, IL: InterVarsity Press, 2007), 13.
48 Labberton, 13.
49 Labberton, 13.

I (Jung Sun Oh) grew up in the conservative mainline South Korean church that emphasizes mainly personal salvation or personal holiness and consequently neglects social sanctification or social holiness. However after attending Candler School of Theology in Atlanta, I slowly realized that my understanding of Christianity and practice of Christian living and social sanctification, especially in connection with social justice ministry, was one-sided. I noticed that the main concern of my faith has been the vertical, exclusive human relationship with God. The horizontal relationships with other human beings and with God's creation, nature, have been neglected. Therefore I have been blinded to the social dimension of salvation and sanctification.

Since 1989, I have made an intentional effort to emphasize and to practice both personal holiness and social holiness, in other words, vertical relationship with God and horizontal relationship with other human beings. As a pastor, I strongly believe that balancing personal and social holiness is the essence of the teaching and living example of Jesus, and of John Wesley as well. I have also emphasized balancing personal and social holiness—the most important element of Christianity, especially of Methodist tradition—both in the order of the worship service, particularly in preaching on Sunday, and in the area of outreach ministries for the poor and the oppressed in our communities.

The Old Testament prophet Micah distilled Israel's call at a critical time: "What does the LORD require of you but to do justice, and to love kindness, and to walk humbly with your God?" (Mic 6:8). God longs for pastors and worship teams who prepare the worship service to be awakened.

Questions for Discussion

1. How does your worship experience stimulate or fail to stimulate your faith in the God of justice?
2. How would you include "balancing personal holiness and social holiness" in your order of worship service regularly?
3. How has your congregation changed over the last ten years with respect to diversity? How has your worship changed as a result—or has it?
4. How does your worship challenge your life with respect to seeking and acting out justice?

5

The Art of Cross-Racial and Cross-Cultural Leadership

As mentioned earlier, the General Board of Higher Education and Ministry (GBHEM) conducted a survey of the leadership styles of United Methodist racial-ethnic pastors who are serving large Caucasian-majority churches.[1] We will call them racial-ethnic, cross-racial, and cross-cultural (RE CR-CC) lead pastors.[2] In this chapter, we will learn from the leadership style of these pastors who have been artfully leading multicultural, multilingual, and multiracial churches

---

1   GBHEM identified seventy-five racial-ethnic pastors serving in churches with a membership of five hundred or more, based on General Council on Finance and Administration (GCFA) data. We had to expand the sample to make a survey relevant for comparison since we identified only twenty racial-ethnic lead pastors who were serving a one thousand or more membership Caucasian-majority church. An online survey was distributed by email to racial-ethnic cross-racial and cross-cultural lead pastors, and we received a 51 percent response rate (thirty-eight complete responses) after initial and three follow-up contacts.

2   The term *lead pastor* was defined by the General Council on Finance and Administration (GCFA) as clergy serving churches with one thousand or more members within The United Methodist Church.

in spite of racial-ethnic and cultural issues, as well as the challenges they face at their current appointments. When asked whether "the call to pastor a large-membership church is distinct from the call to other kinds of pastoral ministries," 57 percent of RE CR-CC lead pastors said yes. The majority of these pastors consider their call as a specialized call that requires a distinct set of skills.

Relationship Building

> "Abide in me as I abide in you. Just as the branch cannot bear fruit by itself unless it abides in the vine, neither can you unless you abide in me. I am the vine, you are the branches. Those who abide in me and I in them bear much fruit, because apart from me you can do nothing." (John 15:4–5)

Pastors who are successfully leading cross-racial and cross-cultural churches are the ones who are able to bring together multicultural perspectives, not only in the formation of their own identity but also in their ministry. By doing so, they demonstrate an inclusive leadership style with cross-racial and cross-cultural competency and sensitivity as bridge builders. Bridge builders not only bring diverse people together based in Christian faith, but also connect people to God.

> Bridge builders bring diverse people together in Christian faith and connect them to God.

An intense and sometimes contentious debate has developed around the identity formation of the Christian church within a culturally and religiously pluralistic context.

The church has been under pressure to negotiate the interpretations of the gospel amid social and cultural diversity. God calls the global church to bring people together in the midst of varied multifaceted perspectives, ideas, and religious preferences. However, it has not been successful in providing a space where discussions on racism, sexism, colonialism, and economic exploitation foster a connection among people who live in a different reality. How can a leader embrace both/and fluidity of a pluralistic culture and maintain a strong sense of self at the same time?

Build Bridges by Living Faith

As mentioned in a previous chapter, the Methodist movement itself represents a church attempting to live as bridge builders, bringing people together through the Word of God. Wesley understood the church as a community of faithful Christians conscientiously living out their faith.[3] Practicing *living faith* was essential in the formation of a visible church. For Wesley, *living faith* should be expressed in and through various spiritual practices, such as Bible study, prayer, fasting, and the Lord's Supper.[4] Likewise, the *living*

---

3   John Wesley interpreted the phrase "a congregation of faithful men" from an Anglican definition of the church (The Anglican Article of Religion, XIX) as "men endued with *living faith*," as we saw in an earlier chapter. "The visible church of Christ is a congregation of faithful men in which the pure Word of God is preached, and the Sacraments be duly administered" (*Book of Discipline 2016*, Article XIII, 62).

4   Gwang Seok Oh, *John Wesley's Ecclesiology: A Study in Its Sources and Development* (Lanham, MD: Scarecrow Press, 2008), 318.

faith of racial-ethnic pastors serving large Caucasian-majority churches is manifested through such things as personal worship, regular spiritual retreats, and spending time with a spiritual director. In fact, our study found that successful RE CR-CC lead pastors especially develop personal virtues, such as "patience," "remembering who they are," and "letting go," which are also significant characteristics of bridge builders. These pastors mentioned that their personal practice of faith—*living faith*—developed their character as strong and resilient Christian leaders who can empathize with the sufferings of others.

According to Randy L. Maddox, Wesley's way of measuring *living faith* is based on a crucial connection between theological reflections and Christian practices.[5] Enhancement of a dialectical relationship between the Word of God and Christian practice is John Wesley's formula for discipleship formation, expressed as *sanctification* in his theology. According to Wesley, "None that is dead to God can be a member of his Church."[6] Therefore, for Wesley, faith is a personal and corporate *living response* to Christ, leading to the imitation of Jesus' life.[7] In other words, the grace of Christ empowers the believer to live a new, transformed life in conformity with Christ. This is Wesley's concept of

---

5   Randy L. Maddox, *Responsible Grace: John Wesley's Practical Theology* (Nashville: Kingswood, 1994).
6   Albert C. Outler, ed., *John Wesley* (New York: Oxford University Press, 1964), 316.
7   Thomas Jackson, ed., *The Works of John Wesley Jackson Edition CD-ROM* (Nashville: Providence House, 1995), 12:151. Hereinafter *Works*.

"practical divinity,"[8] which is a way of pursuing a life of holiness. Wesley's *holiness* means "a renewal of soul in the image of God" by practicing "a complex habit of lowliness, meekness, purity, faith, hope, and love of God and man."[9] A *living faith* is embodied in a *living response* expressed through holiness of life. Wesley was clear that individual holiness of life is crucial to the formation of the church's visible holiness. *Living faith* is the source of Christians' dispositions and acts of love for God and others.[10]

For Wesley, what makes faith a *living faith* is social and contextual consciousness, expressed through a life of holiness that brings diverse people together, closer to God as disciples of Christ. To be a bridge builder between God and God's people, a leader constantly reminds the world, through the narratives of Jesus, that God cares about human suffering. This social consciousness that appreciates human experiences enables the leader to provide a space to bring people closer to each other by sharing God's hospitality, providing hope, and demonstrating compassion to people, especially to the marginalized. It is obvious that these pastors are very conscientious about issues of the oppressed and the disadvantaged because of their own experiences of marginalization.

Likewise, the Methodist movement gave evidence to Wesley's *living faith*, which was expressed in practical divinity as he responded to the social, ethical, economic, and

8   Thomas A. Langford, "John Wesley and Theological Method," in *Rethinking Wesley's Theology for Contemporary Methodism*, ed. Randy L. Maddox (Nashville: Kingswood Books, 1998), 35.
9   Jackson, *Works*, 1:178.
10 Maddox, *Rethinking Wesley's Theology for Contemporary Methodism*, 175 (see chap. 3, n. 6).

religious concerns of England in the mid-eighteenth century. Wesley's consideration of social context and social issues is what makes him a model for any cross-racial and cross-cultural leader to become a bridge builder.

Build Bridges by Preaching the Word of God

For Wesley, Word and sacraments are means of grace, and they are equally important for the formation of the church. Wesley was convinced that preaching "the pure Word of God" facilitates the formation of "the visible church of Christ" by sustaining, refreshing, strengthening, and increasing spiritual life. Theologian Albert C. Outler called Wesley's understanding of preaching "evangelical preaching."[11] Wesley said, "This is the scriptural way, the Methodist way, the true way to preach; that is, 'preaching the gospel—preaching the love of God' and 'preaching the law'—sustains and increases spiritual life in true believers both at once, or both in one."[12]

Likewise, proclaiming the unconditional love of God and God's grace for all people is one of the main themes that RE CR-CC lead pastors preach. As mentioned in chapter 4, preaching nourishes and strengthens the soul by teaching Christians how to walk in Christ in everyday life.[13] Wesley believed that preaching the Word of God "begets faith" in true believers in that it teaches and guides them to live in holiness of life as disciples of Christ.[14] In other words, preaching is a tool for inaugurating a space for openness to "otherness"

---

11 Outler, *John Wesley*, 312, 232.

12 Outler, 232–33.

13 Outler, 233.

14 Outler, 232.

within a Christian community by initiating theological reflection among Christians.

As discussed in chapter 4, preaching is a pivotal area in which Wesley's pragmatism was expressed as he responded to the context of the time. Likewise, RE CR-CC lead pastors use preaching to challenge Christians to practice their faith in their lives by interpreting scripture, nurturing spirituality, conveying information, and studying the Bible. RE CR-CC lead pastors play the role of bridge builders between Christians in the pew and the rest of the world by focusing on social justice and Christian identity issues, such as who we are before God and who we are in relation to others. In so doing, their preaching provides a space for dialogue among Christians to inspire them to practice hope, grace, and unconditional love for all people. For these pastors, preaching the Word of God is the time for challenging Christians to be bridge builders themselves by making a difference and living out the commandment of Jesus Christ.

John Wesley's motto "plain truth for plain people" especially evinces his understanding of the importance of the church's role of bringing people together. Wesley believed that an ideal Methodist preacher must speak plain language.[15] Therefore he started open field preaching, employed lay preachers, and allowed women to preach.[16] Wesley built

---

15 Paul W. Chilcote, *John Wesley and the Women Preachers of Early Methodism* (Metuchen, NJ: Scarecrow Press, 1991), 47.

16 Wesley appointed women as class leaders as early as 1739 and allowed Sarah Crosby to preach in class meetings according to particular circumstances (Jackson, *Works*, 12:353–57). Wesley recognized that women outnumbered men in societies. Sometimes women had to facilitate societies due to the lack of male leaders. As they led societies, women would cross the boundary

relationships with people through these innovative Christian practices. These three initiatives had not been a part of the practices of the Church of England, and Wesley took a risk in responding to people's needs as an expression of his *living faith*. Wesley's practice of preaching with plain language is critical for the leadership quality of a pastor who serves cross-racial and cross-cultural churches, because The UMC as a worldwide church has many multilingual congregations; the art of interpreting biblical knowledge into everyday language is vital in the US context when we consider the multiple levels of English language proficiency, education, social status, and biblical knowledge in a congregation.

RE CR-CC lead pastors practice their faith of bringing together the majority and minority perspectives of society in their ministry. By doing so, they create an inclusive leadership style with cross-cultural competency and sensitivity that represents being bridge builders who not only bring diverse

---

between exhorter and preacher. Influenced by his mother, Susanna Wesley, Wesley acknowledged that women were created in the image of God and accepted their calling to ministry in spite of his belief that women should not be given authority over men (Jackson, *Works*, 11:49, 101). Even though Wesley did not allow women to preach officially until late in his life, he allowed women to visit the sick, to pray, to be exhorters, to be leaders in bands and classes, and to initiate societies (Oh, *John Wesley's Ecclesiology*, 208–11). In 1771, Wesley admitted that some women possess an "extraordinary call," and he accepted that there should be a few exceptions for women to speak in public (Maddox, in Langford, *Rethinking Wesley's Theology*, 35). In 1787, four years before he died, Wesley finally gave official authorization to Sarah Mallet to preach (Chilcote, *John Wesley and the Women Preachers of Early Methodism*, 195).

people together based on Christian faith, but also connect people to God.

Being a Wounded Healer: Listening Is the Beginning of Healing

Let the same mind be in you that was in Christ Jesus, who, though he was in the form of God, did not regard equality with God as something to be exploited, but emptied himself, taking the form of a slave, being born in human likeness. And being found in human form, he humbled himself and became obedient to the point of death—even death on a cross. (Phil 2:5-8)

How can a pastor as a wounded healer in a cross-racial and cross-cultural appointment provide honest and transparent pastoral care? How can a pastor as a wounded healer in a cross-racial and cross-cultural setting build a healthy and vibrant congregation? In short, a pastor in a cross-racial and cross-cultural appointment can be a wounded healer for others from the spirituality based on his or her life experiences, a lived life.

Wounded healer, a term created by psychologist Carl Jung and popularized by Henri Nouwen, comes from the idea that a therapist is compelled to treat patients because he or she is "wounded" as well. In his book *The Wounded Healer*, Nouwen combines creative case studies of ministry with stories from diverse cultures and religious traditions in preparing a new model for ministry. Weaving keen cultural analysis with his psychological and religious insights, Nouwen came up with a balanced and creative theology of service, which begins with the realization of fundamental woundedness in human nature.

Pastors in a cross-racial and cross-cultural setting must be willing to go beyond their professional role and leave themselves open as fellow human beings with the same wounds and suffering—in the image of Christ. In other words, we heal from our own wounds in the process. For example, pastors in cross-racial and cross-cultural appointments live and serve others, with their wounds and sufferings from racism and combinations of racism and sexism, alienation and loneliness, even while recognizing their own woundedness caused by such racial and/or sexual discrimination, alienation, and loneliness.

> Pastors in a cross-racial and cross-cultural setting must be willing to . . . leave themselves open as fellow human beings with the same wounds and suffering.

As pastors in cross-racial and cross-cultural ministry settings, we are called to serve God, our church members, our neighbors, and the world as well. The example and model of our ministry is Jesus, who is a wounded healer. In addition to recognizing their vulnerability to the "isms" of the world, they must also be in the process of their own healing. Their spirituality amid this woundedness and healing can equip and strengthen them to continue to serve God, the local church, the community, and the world.

Biblical Reference

According to Isaiah 53, Jesus was "despised and rejected by others" (v. 3). "Surely he has borne our infirmities and carried our diseases" (v. 4). "But he was wounded for our transgressions, crushed for our iniquities; upon him was the punishment that made us whole, and by his bruises we are healed."(v. 5). "He was oppressed, and he was afflicted, yet he did not open his mouth" (v. 7). "By a perversion of justice he was taken away. Who could have imagined his future? For he was cut off from the land of the living, stricken for the transgression of [God's] people" (v. 8).

As a wounded healer, Jesus preached good news to the poor, proclaimed release to the captives and recovering of sight to the blind, set at liberty those who are oppressed, and announced that the time had come when God would save God's people. Jesus also "healed the sick, fed the hungry, and ate with sinners."[17]

Stress and Loneliness

All pastors wear numerous hats: spiritual leader, worship leader, preacher, teacher, trainer of laity, administrative leader and steward of vision, custodian of institutional integrity, participant in the United Methodist connection, counselor, troubleshooter, mediator, writer, planner, supervisor, wedding/baptism/funeral officiant, fund-raiser, community minister, mission coordinator, outreach ministry coordinator, and so forth. In each role the pastor is expected to be competent, effective, and well informed. Moreover, the pastor is expected to be always cheerful, compassionate and loving, willing, and available, but hardly ever discouraged, depressed, cynical, or hurt. Such a demanding role

---

17 "The Great Thanksgiving for the Season after Pentecost (Ordinary Time, or Kingdomtide)" (liturgy), the website of Discipleship Ministries of The United Methodist Church, accessed March 6, 2018, https://www.umcdiscipleship.org/resources/the-great -thanksgiving-for-the-season-after-pentecost-ordinary-time-or -king.

is overwhelming, especially if a pastor is from a racial-ethnic background different from the majority of the congregation.

Adapting to a new cultural and community environment results in tremendous pressure for most pastors and their families in cross-racial and cross-cultural settings. They can become uncertain about what to do or how to behave. While many pastors suffer from loneliness, pastors in cross-racial and cross-cultural appointments are especially lonely because of demographics and isolation. Often, the pastor and his or her family are the only racial-ethnic minority in the congregation. Many do not have close friends in their neighborhoods. Though they need help dealing with this, they do not seek help. Pastors may be quite close to their congregations, but socially and emotionally they are a great distance away from them.

Racial-Ethnic Clergywomen

The first United Methodist Clergywomen Retention Survey was conducted in 1994 to learn about clergywomen's experience in ministry. In 2011, the Anna Howard Shaw Center at Boston University School of Theology and the Clergy Lifelong Learning Office at GBHEM cosponsored another study by using the same questions to measure progress that women made in The UMC. Among 10,231 active and retired women clergy in the United States, 1,906 women responded to the survey.[18] The study found that UM Clergywomen in the United States serving local churches have increased by

18 Hee A Choi and Jaquelin Blue, "United Methodist Clergywomen Retention Study 2 in the US Context" (Boston: Anna Howard Shaw Center, 2012), http://www.bu.edu/shaw/publications /united-methodist-clergywomen-retention-study-ii-2/.

26.8 percent. Over 95 percent of all UM clergywomen were serving local churches after seventeen years of support and advocacy of the denomination.

The rate of racial-ethnic women serving local churches, in general, leaped between 25 percent (Hispanic) to 100 percent (Native American). 98 percent of African American women were serving local churches, an increase of 39 percent since 1994. This is a result of intentional support from GBHEM for clergywomen by creating racial-ethnic clergywomen associations. For example, the Association of Native American UM Clergywomen was organized in 2008.

Twenty-five percent more of currently married women were serving local churches in 2011 compared to 1994. This could be a result of increased support from their partners and family members and a better understanding of women's leadership roles in church and society. As an example, those who have a clergy partner left local church ministry 23 percent less in 2011.

Fifteen percent of women responded that their main reason for leaving local church ministry was due to lack of support from the hierarchical system of the church; this number has not changed in seventeen years. This figure indicates that the battle of gender equality still resides within the institution of the church primarily.

The number of those who left and returned to local church ministry among racial-ethnic women has increased by 5.8 percent (12 percent in 1994 and 17.8 percent in 2001). This could mean that racial-ethnic women have more ministry options outside of the local church, and the openness of local churches reduces the permanent exit of racial-ethnic clergywomen.

The Rev. Dr. Hee An Choi, director of the Anna Howard Shaw Center and a clinical associate professor of practical theology at Boston University, commented in an interview with M. Garlinda Burton regarding the status of racial-ethnic clergywomen: "I believe the church must look more closely at the appointment system in light of the impact on all women, particularly racial-ethnic women. There are still discrepancies in job security, opportunities to serve larger congregations, and, related to that, to have the salaries that come with upward mobility."[19]

A case in point, there is a small but growing number of women now serving as lead pastors of one-thousand-plus members. There were 64 women leading large United Methodist churches in 2008; recent numbers found 137 women senior pastors of large churches. However, only a few women of color occupy these pulpits, and the denomination has yet to elect an Asian or Native American woman as bishop—all signs that the church still struggles with institutional racism, sexism, work-family stress that affects women disproportionately, and the "economic stratification" within the United Methodist clergy system.[20] As we saw above, clergywomen have faced barriers to fulfilling their potential, but they have turned obstacles into transformational energy, which, in turn, has created a new form of leadership in the church. Even though women have made great strides as leaders not only in social, economic, and political arenas but also in religious sectors, disapproval of their leadership, systemic exploitation of their

---

19 Burton, "Women Pastors Growing in Numbers," UMNS, Nashville, TN, March 20, 2014. http://www.umc.org/news-and-media /women-pastors-growing-in-numbers.
20 Park and Willhauck, eds., *Breaking Through the Stained Glass Ceiling.*

labor, silencing of their voices, and unrealistic role expectations still marginalize women from leadership positions.

Martin Luther King Jr. as a Wounded Healer

Pastors in cross-racial and cross-cultural appointments can learn insights from Rev. Dr. Martin Luther King Jr.'s idea of "the Beloved Community," one of four parts of what is known today as the "King philosophy," a philosophy of nonviolence that guided King's strategy for the civil rights movement of the 1950s and 1960s. Fellowship of Reconciliation founder Josiah Royce (1855–1916) originated the term "Beloved Community," but it was King, who later became part of the Fellowship, who made the term popular. For King, the Beloved Community was not a promise of Utopia, but a realistic goal that "could be accomplished by a critical mass of people committed and trained in the . . . methods of nonviolence."[21] See www.thekingcenter.org/king-philosophy for more information on the Beloved Community.

Resource

> We affirm all persons as equally valuable in the sight of God. We therefore work toward societies in which each person's value is recognized, maintained, and strengthened. . . . We deplore acts of hate or violence against groups or persons based on race, color, national origin, ethnicity, age, gender, disability, status, economic condition, sexual orientation, gender identity or religious affiliation. . . .

---

21 The King Center, "The King Philosophy," thekingcenter.org, accessed March 6, 2018, http://www.thekingcenter.org/king -philosophy#sub4.

Rights of Racial and Ethnic Persons—Racism is the combination of the power to dominate by one race over the races and a value system that assumes that the dominant race is innately superior to the others. Racism includes both personal and institutional racism. Personal racism is manifested through the individual expressions, attitudes, and/or behaviors that accept the assumptions of a racist value system and that maintain the benefits of this system. Institutional racism is the established social pattern that supports implicitly or explicitly, the racist value system. Racism, manifested as sin, plagues and hinders our relationship with Christ, inasmuch as it is antithetical to the gospel itself. In many cultures white persons are granted unearned privileges and benefits that are denied to persons of color. We oppose the creation of a racial hierarchy in any culture. Racism breeds racial discrimination. We define racial discrimination as the disparate treatment and lack of full access and equity in resources, opportunities, and participation in the Church and in society based on race or ethnicity.

Therefore, we recognize racism as sin and affirm the ultimate and temporal worth of all persons. We rejoice in the gifts that particular ethnic histories and cultures bring to our total life. We commit as the Church to move beyond symbolic expressions and representative models that do not challenge unjust systems of power and access. (*Book of Discipline 2016*, Social Principles: The Social Community, ¶162)

Biblical Reference

God created humans in God's image. Therefore, theologically speaking, there is only one race, the human race. Caucasians, African Americans, Africans, Asians, Asian Pacific Islanders, Indians, Hispanics, Arabs, and Jews are all God's children:

> So God created humankind in [God's] image, in the image of God [God] created them; male and female [God] created them. (Gen 1:27)

God does not show partiality or favoritism; therefore, neither should we:

> For the LORD your God is God of gods and Lord of lords, the great God, mighty and awesome, who is not partial and takes no bribe, who executes justice for the orphan and the widow, and who loves the strangers, providing them food and clothing. (Deut 10:17-18)

> Then Peter began to speak to them: "I truly understand that God shows no partiality, but in every nation anyone who fears him and does what is right is acceptable to him." (Acts 10:34-35)

> For God shows no partiality. (Rom 2:11)

Jesus commands us to love one another as he loves us, regardless of race:

> "I give you a new commandment, that you love one another. Just as I have loved you, you also should love one another." (John 13:34)

Therefore we are to love our neighbors, including people of different races, as ourselves:

You do well if you really fulfill the royal law according to the scripture, "You shall love your neighbor as
yourself." (James 2:8)

In Christ we all are sisters and brothers:

There is no longer Jew or Greek, there is no longer
slave or free, there is no longer male and female; for
all of you are one in Christ Jesus." (Gal 3:28)

Being a Stereotype Breaker: A Vulnerable Trailblazer

Do not be conformed to this world, but be transformed by the renewing of your minds, so that you
may discern what is the will of God—what is good and
acceptable and perfect. (Rom 12:2)

According to GBHEM's study, racial-ethnic pastors who
are serving large Caucasian-majority churches are breaking stereotypes, not only by their presence but also by their
skills. When asked about the leadership styles, the pastors
felt their congregations' values best aligned with *Nurturing,
Servant Leader,* and *Democratic.* When asked how often they
utilize certain leadership styles compared to white lead pastors, they reported that they are more "often" and "always"
collaborative, equipping, directive, confident, creative, nurturing, energetic, adaptive, charismatic, delegating, servant leaders, persuasive, democratic, compassionate, and
prophetic. They are less ("never" or "rarely") authoritarian
and more ("always") decisive. When asked how they would
respond if a parishioner verbally attacked them in a meeting, 69.4 percent of RE CR-CC lead pastors said they would
"calmly address" the matter, compared to 31.1 percent of
white lead pastors. Twenty-five percent of RE CR-CC lead

pastors who responded said that they would "pray about it," compared to 8.3 percent of white lead pastors. (More white pastors would either defend their actions or make jokes out of the situation than racial-ethnic pastors.) (See pp. 7–8.)

These findings are breaking stereotypes about racial-ethnic leaders, such as "African-American males are loud and rough"; "Asian-American leaders are too authoritative and rigid"; and "racial-ethnic leaders are less effective in administration." For example, according to my research for *Creating Christian Community Through the Cross-Racial Appointment*, the stereotype about racial-ethnic pastors being less effective was more evident among respondents. In that research, some of them said, "Yes, the church should be a racially inclusive community, but the appointment of pastors is a different matter," and "Ability is more important than being an inclusive community. We should accept pastors by ability, not by their color."[22]

Racial-ethnic CR-CC lead pastors are conscientious about developing leadership skills. Of these pastors, 68 percent developed their leadership skills through a formal leadership training program, compared to 50.5 percent of white lead pastors who responded to the same question. However, fewer RE CR-CC lead pastors indicated that they learned from a role model (65.8 percent), compared to 67 percent of white lead pastors. This makes sense considering there were only seventy-five RE CR-CC lead pastors who serve Caucasian-majority churches with a membership of five hundred or more in 2014. Furthermore, their ordination history is shorter; for example, racial-ethnic women only

---

22 Park, "Creating Christian Community through the Cross-Racial Appointment" (see intro, n. 6).

started being appointed in any number in the late 1970s in the United States. Therefore, these pastors are trailblazers and lifelong learners, as they practice their leadership in large church settings. This is why the network of racial-ethnic cross-racial and cross-cultural lead pastors is crucial for their leadership development. RE CR-CC lead pastors are called to a ministry of vulnerability; their presence and leadership style shatter ethnocentrism and open up new possibilities of God's revelation. Their vulnerability challenges the congregation and many times leads them to a spiritual transformation toward a new and different future for the church.

Being a Committed Educator: A Lifelong Learner

Do not remember the former things, or consider the things of old. I am about to do a new thing; now it springs forth, do you not perceive it? I will make a way in the wilderness and rivers in the desert. (Isa 43:18–19)

Racial-ethnic cross-racial and cross-cultural lead pastors understand the importance of education to narrow the gap between exclusion and inclusion. The research showed that these pastors displayed a strong desire to achieve higher education not only for themselves but also for the congregation. It makes sense that these pastors see themselves serving the church as highly committed educators for inclusion of diversity. Not only do 40.5 percent of them have doctoral-level educations, but the majority of them also understand their role as theological educators in the church. For example, a few mentioned the importance of providing continuing education on cross-racial and cross-cultural ministry and of providing critical biblical interpretation through their preaching.

Overall, the research represents RE CR-CC lead pastors as fluent and versatile adaptive leaders willing to take a risk and start new things. They are socially and contextually conscientious about deepening their faith. They continue to learn and develop their leadership skills and participate in their own spiritual formation. The survey witnesses that these pastors are adaptive leaders with the skills necessary to serve cross-racial and cross-cultural appointments. For example, more racial-ethnic pastors serving large Caucasian-majority churches have served as Board of Ordained Ministry chairpersons, extension ministers, and associate pastors. Yet only 13.2 percent of them served as district superintendents, compared to 17 percent of white lead pastors. Almost half of racial-ethnic pastors are second-career pastors. They bring the skills to lead multi-staff congregations with stronger financial management skills and adapt themselves according to different contexts, while only one-third of white lead pastors came into ministry as a second career. The church is blessed to have these experienced racial-ethnic leaders who utilize their expertise.

More of the racial-ethnic pastors who are serving large Caucasian majority churches "always" lead change by equipping and educating others (white pastors 10.9 percent versus RE CR-CC pastors 32.4 percent), and 28.6 percent of RE CR-CC lead pastors "often and always" make decisions by taking a vote, compared to 1.1 percent of white lead pastors. This indicates that racial-ethnic pastors skillfully involve others in a decision-making process to leave little room for argument or conflicts.

According to the GBHEM study, more RE CR-CC lead pastors (67 percent) responded that their confidence level in financial management has improved since they became large church lead pastors. This is a result of their constant learning and developing financial management skills. Even though they responded that they enjoy working on church finances (42.9 percent), they showed less confidence in financial management (65.8 percent) when compared to white lead pastors (87.2 percent). These findings correlate with white lead women pastors' responses in 2010; that is, that they enjoy working on finances but express less confidence than white male lead pastors. One racial-ethnic lead pastor mentioned that he relies on the expertise of laity who are financial professionals. The evidence convinces us that an attitude of and commitment to lifelong learning contributes to being an effective cross-racial and cross-cultural leader.

Being Able to Disrupt Marginality

> The spirit of the Lord GOD is upon me, because the LORD has anointed me; he has sent me to bring good news to the oppressed, to bind up the brokenhearted, to proclaim liberty to the captives, and release to the prisoners; to proclaim the year of the LORD's favor, and the day of vengeance of our God; to comfort all who mourn; to provide for those who mourn in Zion—to give them a garland instead of ashes, the oil of gladness instead of mourning, the mantle of praise instead of a faint spirit. (Isa 61:1-3)

As we learned from chapter 3, *han* is the universal experience of all who have been excluded from social, economic, cultural, political, and religious access, regardless of their race/ethnicity, gender, or culture. However, leaders who are able to minister to people cross-racially and cross-culturally are those who have turned their *han* into a "will for life" and "energy for evolution" to promote constructive change. Their experiences of *han* have enabled them to be other-centered by "disrupting the marginality" in a society.[23]

"Disrupting marginality" is a practice of faith that demands aggressive self-giving based on keeping one's integrity of faith. Jesus demonstrated the concept of aggressive self-giving by his sacrifice on the cross. His passion demonstrated a way of transcending the experience of sacrifice through aggressive self-giving to humanity (Heb 9:25-10:4). His radical self-giving brought a possibility of new life to all human beings. This transformation was possible because Jesus understood the intention of God for his life—his call from God to extend God's grace for all humanity (John 17:1-5). Racial-ethnic cross-racial and cross-cultural lead pastors as cultural and relational beings can understand their call to transform their tragic experiences, such as racial prejudice and discrimination, into a foundation for aggressive self-giving so that they are able to "disrupt the marginality" of others. The theological concept of aggressive self-giving is essential to being an inclusive church when many Christians find it hard to embrace "otherness" due to their inability to fathom what it means to sacrifice themselves for others. Aggressive self-giving puts oneself in the center of giving willingly and subjectively.

> Leaders who are able to minister to people cross-racially and cross-culturally are those who have turned their *han* into a "will for life" and "energy for evolution."

---

23 Brock, "Cooking Without Recipes," 135–40 (see chap. 2, n. 22).

Han experiences force RE CR-CC lead pastors to embrace "otherness" consciously. "Otherness" is expressed by the dominant culture in order to conquer or polarize by promoting linguistic and cultural segregation. "Otherness" involves marginality, according to Korean American theologian Jung Yong Lee. Lee asserts that "marginality" is a condition for discipleship.[24] In terms of disrupting marginality by deconstructing a power structure and redistributing power, Lee contends that the church's inclination "to dominate and exclude others because of their race, gender, or class" is not the church of Jesus Christ. He calls this church "pseudo-Christianity."[25] While "pseudo-Christianity" seeks dominance, Lee continues, true Christianity seeks decentralization and the distribution of power. Lee is convinced that the very inclination to seek the center within us is the source of oppression by others.[26]

Feminist theologian Kathleen Sands seeks a pluralistic approach to understanding the complexity of power in her book *Escape from Paradise*. Sands calls the human experiences of suffering *tragedy*. Tragedy is "the inevitability of our involvement in evil." Tragic experiences help Christians become aware of the collusion of social and religious institutions. "Tragic consciousness" is an awareness of the human "enigma of suffering,"[27] for example, RE CR-CC lead pastors' "tragic" experience of *han*—through racial and cultural discrimination—which raises their "tragic consciousness" toward

24 Jung Young Lee, *Marginality* (Minneapolis: Fortress Press, 1995), 118.
25 "Pseudo-Christianity" refers to a church that seeks a position of "centrality." Lee, 120.
26 Lee, 150.
27 Lee, 64-65.

other human beings' suffering. Their "tragic consciousness" is displayed in their preaching, sacramental life, and practices of faith. It reinforces their practice of aggressive self-giving toward others; by doing so, they are "disrupting marginality."

Historically Jesus sought to disrupt marginality by self-emptying, or *kenosis* (Phil 2:5-8), which was possible because of his clear "tragic consciousness" in terms of understanding humanity. Jesus demonstrated his self-realization and self-fulfillment by sharing his marginal experiences as a way of understanding others. Jesus also demonstrated a new concept. When Christians empty themselves, they become filled with a new understanding of self and others; their marginal experiences turn into "tragic consciousness," which paves a way to connect others who are struggling. This experience cannot be ignored, but instead leads to a greater capacity for compassion for the pain and suffering of others. The key is the recognition of "tragic consciousness" created within believers through Jesus Christ. This recognition forces us to seek solidarity to overcome any form of oppression. "Tragic consciousness" within the disciples of Christ enables them to see themselves as subjects of liberation who need to be liberated from the centralist inclination that resists theological, ideological, and cultural differences.

Catholic theologian William Cavanaugh avers that Christians' "tragic consciousness" is crucial in the life of the church if the church is going to "disrupt the marginality" of people in society. He argues that when the church is unable to disrupt the tragedy of unjust forces, it becomes a "disappearing church" without tragic consciousness.[28] Therefore, he urges

---

28 William T. Cavanaugh, *Torture and Eucharist* (Malden, MA: Black-well Publishing, 2003), 177-97.

that tragic consciousness be at the core of being the church. Tragic consciousness is a gift that RE CR-CC lead pastors bring to the church, especially when the church is called to minister to the underprivileged, who are further marginalized due to neo-capitalistic globalization. For example, a tragic experience of discrimination due to racism raised RE CR-CC lead pastors' tragic consciousness toward other human beings, which is reflected in all they do. This is how marginality is disrupted.

Discipleship happens when human suffering, *han*, is acutely addressed in light of the gospel. Disrupting the marginality of people by "tragic consciousness" is central for being an effective leader serving a cross-racial and cross-cultural church.

Questions for Discussion

1. What do you have to do differently to be a bridge builder for God's creation?
2. What is true about you being a "wounded healer"?
3. How does a cross-racial and cross-cultural leader contribute to the life of a church or your organization?
4. How do you know that you or somebody you know would have "tragic consciousness"?
5. What needs to be said about cross-racial and cross-cultural pastors' leadership style that has not been said here?

6

Reflections of Racial-Ethnic Clergy Serving in Caucasian-Majority Churches

The following essays are by racial-ethnic clergy who are serving large Caucasian-majority churches. These writings express their perspectives on creating a multicultural faith community, joys and struggles in cross-racial and cross-cultural ministry, and faithful responses to a prophetic call to serve in such a context in spite of their vulnerability.

Cross-Racial and Cross-Cultural Ministry and the Great Commission

Rev. Dr. Kevin James

The church has been given the commission to go forth and make disciples of all nations (Matt 28:16-20). We know it as the Great Commission, and as the late Bishop Cornelius Henderson said, "It is not called the Great Suggestion." Jesus gave the *commission*, not the *suggestion,* to make disciples.

Bishop Noah Moore told the wonderful old story of a crowd that went to the hilltop to pray for rain. Drought had devastated the area. Crops and cattle had died, and the land was parched. As the desperate crowd went up the hill, an

African American woman joined them. She had a raincoat, rain hat, rain boots, and an umbrella. She looked silly, so someone asked her, "What are you doing with all this stuff? Don't you know it has not rained in weeks?" Her response was priceless: "Why are you climbing up this hill, anyway? If I ask God for rain, I expect a downpour!"

The key to manifesting the power of Christ in your life is to expect something to happen. Unfortunately, many of us miss the power of Christ in our lives, because our spiritual imaginations are closed and we do not expect anything to happen. This is not some principle of positive thinking; it is a simple spiritual truth. The power of Christ will not move within us unless we awaken and earnestly desire to be moved by it. Christ will not force his power on us anymore than he will force his will on us. Christ loves us above all, and there is no such thing as forced love.

Let me share excerpts from my book entitled *Guess Who's Coming to Church*. The book title derives from the well-known American movie *Guess Who's Coming to Dinner* (1967). The movie is about an interracial relationship and is one of my favorites, including actors Sidney Poitier, Spencer Tracy, and Katherine Hepburn. I truly believe it is one of the best teaching models related to race relations.

In that story, African American Sidney Poitier plays John, a gentleman dating a Caucasian young woman named Joey, and John is about to meet her parents for the first time. Initially Joey has a conversation with her mother about John, letting her mother know they plan to marry, and then mother and daughter arrange a dinner so that Joey's father, Matt, can meet John as well. When the father, Matt, walks into his home he realizes something is going on. His reaction is swift and direct, saying "What in the hell is going on?"

When Matt realizes this is the guy his daughter is in love with, John says to Joey's parents, "I'm not asking your permission to love your daughter. I love her and would do anything for her. I just wanted you to know that."

The correlation between the storyline and the church is that when a minority pastor is appointed to a Caucasian congregation, or a Caucasian pastor is appointed to a minority congregation, there are going to be some who embrace the appointment and some who are not sure why this is happening in their setting. There will be some who will say, "What is going on?" Some will say, "No. I'm going to sit this out. I'm not ready for it. I don't know why it is being done to our church. We didn't ask for this to be done. What are the other people in the community going to say about what is happening at our church?"

The number one issue that is considered by the bishop and the church cabinet in an appointment is, how is this going to fit into the life of the membership of the church? Will the church lose its identity? Will it lose its history? Will it lose its traditions? For many people, when they first hear, "Well, you are going to receive a minority pastor and undergo a cross-cultural experience," they say, "Oh, Lord, we hope we can survive." But it is not about surviving; it is about thriving in the midst of this experience. Your church can be highlighted in a different way in the community.

I believe that the reactions in the movie are examples of what occurs in churches, academic settings, work environments, and communities. Here are three elements in preparation for a cross-cultural experience such as this.

The Pastor

Some may wonder if there is a certain type of pastor who is best-suited for a cross-cultural appointment. First, such a pastor will ideally be one who is comfortable in his or her own skin. He or she will understand that they are going into a situation where all the landmines have not been dug up; where bigotries, hatreds, and racism may be present, which may have been dormant up to now but are going to surface. As a pastor you must remember: don't allow the critics to define your ministry and your life. That is very important. There are going to be critics and you cannot allow them to determine how you minister to and interact with others. You have been called to go forth and to share the good news, and that is your commitment. So, you must keep that forever before you. As my son says, "You must believe in what you are doing."

When I was called to preach I was not called only to preach to African Americans. I was called to preach the gospel of Jesus Christ. There is a phrase in the church: whosoever will, let them come. So when you have that calling in your life, you look to minister to all people and you do not segregate by saying, "I can't minister to this group of people here or those people over there—Jews, Samaritans, blacks, whites." You are sent to minister out of your own ethos and to share out of your own day-to-day experiences.

The Pastor's Family

The pastoral family is one of the keys to a successful cross-cultural appointment and shares the joys, celebrations, and frustrations of this enriched encounter.

There are countless joys and celebrations that I have experienced. However, there are two sides to every coin, in this case both negative and positive experiences. Allow me to share with you one unfortunate experience.

In 2002, the Clearwater Police Department was in search of four males who had just committed a crime. They were in an SUV described by the police dispatcher as bronze, maroon/beige, gray, beige, or silver in color, according to the police report. Police were all over. I was driving my maroon-colored Tahoe and had just picked up a friend, Stanley Boyd. He, along with my wife, Linda, and my son, Kevin Jr., were going to Orlando for the Bethune-Cookman/Florida A&M Classic football game. Before I go on the road to travel, I always pray; therefore, we stopped by the Clearwater Country Club to pray before our departure.

Shortly after we started our trip, we were stopped by a police officer and soon after a convoy of officers arrived. They pulled out their guns and ordered us out of the vehicle. They handcuffed Stanley Boyd and myself and searched us. It wasn't until I was on the ground, guns pointed at us, that one of the officers said, "These are not the suspects." Of course, it would have been easy for even Stevie Wonder or Ray Charles to have shared that insight with them! We didn't fit the descriptions. They really made a very critical mistake that continues to haunt my family to this day. It was a sense of disappointment, and to me, it was clearly a case of racial profiling—still it does exist. For those who don't want me to talk about it, don't want to hear it, maybe they are making excuses. Perhaps until it happens to them, they will not be able to acknowledge that racial profiling still occurs.

We asked to speak with the Clearwater chief of police, who is white, but he did not come that night. It was almost two weeks after I filed a complaint that he even acknowledged the incident. We were going back and forth with letters, and I was just requesting to meet with him. His answer was that they just made an honest mistake. Nothing happened, so let's move on.

A year later, I sought legal help. At that point, the current city manager, an African American to whom I had sent copies of all my letters addressed to the chief, decided city officials would meet with us to apologize officially. But, they still couldn't see or admit that they had done anything wrong. I asked the chief, "If I had your gun and I drew that gun on your wife, what would you do?" And he couldn't answer that. I said, "See, that has never happened to you, so you don't know my situation or my experience. You haven't walked in my shoes."

I believe these kinds of experiences are relevant to the topic of race relations in our society. I have lived through, deeply felt, and come out on the other side of them.

Church Leadership

The church leadership must prepare itself and step up to teach and help other people in the congregation when embracing a cross-cultural appointment. It will be a fascinating moment when the leadership rises to the occasion and says to other people that they are going to work together regarding this new appointment. It is an opportunity to learn from the new pastor, learn about his or her family, and welcome a new day, a new experience.

One of the first reactions for many people in a congregation receiving a cross-cultural appointment is to say, "Why my church? Why is this happening?" The answer to that is to remember that it is not "our" church. We do take allegiance and a sense of ownership when it comes to the church. But it is Christ's church, and Christ is pushing us and molding, shaping, and developing us in our faith. This is a part of the stages of development where Christ works within us to develop us and to make us what we claim to be: Christians. So, the question to ask is, "Why not my church?" When we say, "Why my church?" we are really saying that we are concerned that this has happened to *my house*. Guess who's coming to my church, and why? "Why is this person coming here?" It goes back to the movie. "Why is this happening now in my home, in my life, in my family's life? How am I to respond to this?"

It reminds us of the mission and ministry of the church. It reminds us who is the owner of the church and it also reminds us of our responsibility in the church. Even though it seems as if there are some growing pains, we can step up to the plate and exercise and demonstrate our faith while still asking questions. The questions will be answered as we fulfill this appointment. You cannot immediately say, "Here are the answers," unless you respond like the general church, and I'm speaking of The United Methodist Church, by saying that our church is open to inclusiveness, and we match the gifts and graces of all pastors and leaders.

Some members of the church will naturally want to know, "What should I expect with this? How is this going to be different for my church than what it has been?" Well, it is going to be very different, because, more than likely, the leadership style will be different, the preaching will be different, mannerisms will be different. There will be a different sense of conversation. But what is common ground, what comes together, is that we will all focus on what we have been called to do as the body of Christ and the mission and ministry of the Church. That will not change. The core components of carrying out the biblical message will not change. You are dealing with the personality of the person. The method of presentation may change, but you and the church are still going in the same direction, you will still have the same focus, and you still need to have the same mission.

As the senior pastor of Palm Coast United Methodist Church in the Florida Annual Conference, this passage is present in our context daily. Our congregation is a diverse parish with forty countries represented in fellowship. Here's a comment from one of our members:

> As a "snow bird" from Ohio, I visited several churches in Palm Coast including PCUMC prior to the appointment of Dr. Kevin M. James Sr. After my arrival, I soon joined and became an engaged member. I am thankful that soon after, my husband did the same. Our decision to join this church as active members is much to the credit of our pastor due to [his] delivery and communication skills. Every Sunday, the message is scriptural, current, relatable, and memorable. In short, I remember and hopefully can apply the message. [We also appreciate our pastor's] leadership style and personal interaction. He recognizes the talents of others and fosters the application of those skills in church ministries. He gives you a personal identity and makes the church experience feel warm and inviting. Finally, I truly see him as a servant leader.

In closing, I would like to share this poem from an unknown author, entitled "Don't Quit."

When things go wrong, as they sometimes will,
When the road you're trudging seems all uphill,
When the funds are low and the debts are high
And you want to smile but you have to sigh,
When care is pressing you down a bit,

Rest, if you must, but just don't quit.
So stick to the fight when you're hardest hit—
It's when things seem worst that you must not quit.

Why? Because we have the MVP on our side—Jesus Christ. In the words of the hymnologist, Alfred Henry Ackley,

I serve a risen savior
He's in the world today.
I know that He is living,
Whatever men may say.
I see His hand of mercy,
I hear His voice of cheer,
and just the time I need Him,
He's always near.
He lives! He lives!

May God bless you in Jesus' Name.

Who Is My Neighbor? (Luke 10:25-37 NRSV)

Rev. Don Lee

I currently serve as the lead pastor of FUMC in Denton, Texas, a large downtown church in a county seat community. I come from a multicultural family. My wife Susan is Caucasian. I'm Japanese American. Our biological daughter's name is Clari. And then there's my adopted son, Chris, from Mexico. My extended family includes Italian, Argentinian, Spanish, Filipino, and Japanese lineage. As I've thought about how our world is changing and the conflicts this change brings, I think of Jesus' parable of the Good Samaritan and how it offers us a way to be together.

The parable begins, "What must I do to inherit eternal life?" Jesus throws the question back at the lawyer, forcing him to defend his own competence. The lawyer recites from the Shema, a prayer adapted from Deuteronomy 6:4-9, which every orthodox Jew repeats twice daily. The first line reads, "Sh'ma Yisra'eil Adonai Eloheinu Adonai echad." "Hear, Israel, the Lord is our God, the Lord is One." It continues, "And you shall love the Lord your God with all your heart, soul, strength, and mind."

The lawyer adds words from Leviticus 19:18, "You shall love your neighbor as yourself." Jesus responds, "Do this and you will live." In other words, when it comes to life in God's Kingdom, doing is key to life in God's Kingdom come on Earth. "But who is my neighbor?" asks the lawyer. In other words, "Who am I required to love?" In verse 30, Jesus replies, "A man was going down from Jerusalem to Jericho . . ."

According to The New Interpreter's Bible Commentary, the Jericho road that ran between Jerusalem and Jericho was notoriously dangerous, descending nearly 3300 feet in 17 miles. The path wound its way through mountainous terrain, making it an ideal place for robbers to lie in wait for potential victims. Anyone familiar with this stretch of road knew just how dangerous it was to travel alone. We know almost nothing about our traveler who falls prey to these dangers, who he is, where he is from, or his reason for travel. The only thing we do know is that he is a man and that he demonstrates a serious lack of judgment. This is where many women in my church nod their heads in agreement. Ironically, each character in the story demonstrates a lack of judgment.

Jesus tells us a Priest sees the man and passes by on the other side. Priests served at the Jerusalem temple offering sacrifices to God on behalf of the people, and they were

known to be some of the wealthiest members of Jewish society. Thus, some biblical writers argue the parable's original
audience would not have assumed this priest was on foot.
According to the law, if a priest found a corpse while on a
journey, he had a duty to bury it. The fact that the man was
still alive absolved the priest of any responsibility. So while
the Priest did not do the compassionate thing, he did meet
the requirements of the law, the working premise being, "As
long as I do the least of what's expected of me, I'm good."
I've been trying to define love in terms of "giving the least of
what's expected." If you are sitting by someone you know,
turn to them and say with the utmost sincerity, "You can
always count on me to give you the least of what's expected."
Is this what love looks like? Doing the least of what's expected
of you? It's been my experience that the people who are truly
happy in life are not the ones who give the least of what's
expected. Generosity is a spiritual practice that makes loving God and neighbor a priority in our lives.

Next we are told a Levite sees the man. He too passes by
on the other side. Levites had a special call to assist priests
in the temple. They served as gatekeepers, musicians, and
teachers and were required to take part in the mitzvah, the
Jewish commandment to do "good" to others. So why did
he not stop? Unlike the priest, the Levite would have had no
pack animal to carry the traveler. Carrying the injured traveler would have slowed him down, and with night falling, his
exposure to danger only increased. "What might it cost me
if I stopped?" Have you ever thought that while passing by
someone in need?

The Priest and the Levite both resist the pull of heart and
conscience, and reason away doing the loving thing. While
they knew the law in their heads, they didn't know it down in

their hearts. Jesus is quoting Hosea 6:6 when he says, "Go and learn what this means, 'I desire mercy, not sacrifice.'" Not only did the Priest and Levite fail to consider what it would cost this traveler if he did not stop, each failed to consider what it would cost him to keep going! When you ignore suffering your soul becomes cold and uncaring.

Now a Samaritan happens upon the wounded traveler. Two actions identify him as a neighbor: First, he came near. Modern day Samaritans are the descendants of Jews left behind during the Assyrian Exile. In Jesus' day both Samaritan and Jew believed the other had deviated from the true faith. Given centuries of mutual hatred and distrust, it's easy to see why the lawyer debating Jesus would not have considered a Samaritan his neighbor. To Jesus' original audience, the priest and Levite were the good guys, and the Samaritans were the bad guys. The literal meaning of the word "neighbor," *plēsion* in the original language, *means to be near.* So the answer to the question, "Who is the neighbor?" has to be the Samaritan. Both the Priest and the Levite widen the distance between themselves and the man in the ditch. Only the Samaritan comes near. As an old Arab proverb puts it, "To have a good neighbor, you must be one."

The second action that identifies the Samaritan as a neighbor is that he "took pity." Have you ever been the answer to someone's prayer? In the Bible when God acts, God does so most often through people. If you've ever seen someone in need and you were moved to help, you were being God's answer to their prayer. Compassion is our cooperation with the Holy Spirit to further the kingdom of God on earth. The Good Samaritan is a kingdom parable. It attempts to answer the question, "What is the kingdom of God like?" Jesus is saying, "This is what God's kingdom looks like: Where even the one who considers you an enemy is moved by compassion, and stops to help." But the story doesn't end with seeing. It ends with doing. The Samaritan went, poured, bandaged, put, brought, and cared. Each action only increases the tension setting us up for Jesus' question: "Which of these three, do you think, was a neighbor?" The lawyer can't even bring himself to identify the Samaritan by name. He responds, "The one who showed him mercy."

While in seminary I worked the night shift at a publishing house. When Andrew, a coworker, found out I was in seminary he took great delight in trying to embarrass me. He was rude, mean, and even tried to get me fired. I begged my wife to let me quit. She replied, "You can't. We need the money. Besides," she added, "why don't you try the love of Jesus you are always preaching about." So I decided to do just that. I forgave Andrew's rude comments and efforts to embarrass me, but after three months nothing had changed. Then when Andrew's wife asked him for a divorce and sued for full custody of their daughter, I was the person that Andrew came to for support. The kind of love that evidences the arrival of God's kingdom is not convenient or cheap or easy. It's over the top. And here's what the Good Samaritan discovered, that in reaching out to help someone else, the Samaritan was blessed with joy.

I mentioned at the start my son was adopted from Mexico. All children deserve loving parents. But I confess. Initially I was concerned I would not be able to love an adopted child as much as I loved my biological daughter. All my worry vanished the first time I held Chris in my arms and looked down into his face. I instantly fell in love with him. Adopting Chris is one of the best things my wife and I have ever done. He is truly a blessing to us, and I can't imagine my life without him being in it.

The key to life in God's kingdom on Earth is not so much in the saying but in the doing. During the season of Lent, my church partnered with St. James African Methodist Episcopal Church in Denton to rebuild their church. We renovated the kitchen of this historic church, replaced sheetrock, and textured the sanctuary and fellowship hall walls. We also repaired and repainted the exterior of the building. For Easter, FUMC Denton designated its offering for our sister Methodist church in Russia, Saratov, the second most successful Methodist church in that country. There are some in Russia who consider the United States an enemy, and some in the United States who feel the same toward Russia. All I know is that we all need Jesus in our lives. And the question is, what are you and I going to do about it?

The Art of CR-CC Leadership

Rev. Dr. Jon E. McCoy

Cross-racial cross-cultural (CR-CC) appointments are becoming more common in The United Methodist Church. CR-CC appointments represent unique opportunities for the Church to facilitate key conversations and the development of significant relationships that are not commonly observed in other settings or institutions. These appointments are sometimes accompanied by numerous unspoken assumptions by both clergy members and members of the congregation. These assumptions can be quite wide ranging and often reflect the exceptional nature of CR-CC exposure. Unfortunately, because many of these assumptions are based upon limited information or experiences, there is often extreme reluctance to engage in candid dialogue, in an attempt to avoid embarrassing or awkward conversations. As a result, the common patterns and pathways of decision making, administration, and preaching—the essential roles of the pastor—are sometimes obfuscated in layers of misinformation.

It seems to be rarely acknowledged that while CR-CC appointments typically involve ethnic minorities serving predominantly European American churches, the clergy have often had more CR-CC experiences in other settings than the members of the congregation. In other words, ethnic minorities and women usually have had many experiences being the only member of their ethnic group or gender in vocational, recreational, or other settings. As an African American man serving a CR-CC appointment in a relatively affluent suburb, I am accustomed to being one of a few if not the only African American present in most communal settings. Not only in the church but also in restaurants, stores, government offices, and other businesses, I frequently am the only African American present as an employee or patron. In these instances, my presence is particularly noticeable. However, because there are so few African Americans present, it does not take long for the word to spread regarding my identity as the new pastor of the local United Methodist church.

In the church setting, the pastor is not only the primary executive but also the public face of the church. The church is often associated with and/or identified by the pastor. In CR-CC appointments, some dimensions of the contrast between the congregation and the pastor are often obvious, but the contrast is difficult to discuss. The label CR-CC implicitly emphasizes the differences between the clergy person and the congregation. The label CR-CC also seems to suggest that the contrast is along both racial and cultural lines. However, neither the racial differences nor the cultural differences require highlighting or emphasis. Certainly, there can be appointments in which there are no racial differences. However, the cultural differences can be the source of the difficulties. The church is both a worldwide institution (that proclaims Jesus as the singular leader) and a carefully nurtured affinity group. Although the triune Godhead is undisputed, the impact of the pastor upon the identity and ministry of the local congregation is sometimes debated. We proclaim that we are united; we sing songs that celebrate our identity as brothers and sisters. However, in CR-CC appointments, we sometimes emphasize differences. This emphasis on differences can be seen as the source of potential conflict rather than the foundation of phenomenal synergy.

CR-CC appointments often create an excited buzz similar to the walk to Emmaus in which the unrecognized, resurrected Jesus quizzed the disciples about their heated conversation. Those disciples were incredulous. Cleopas asked Jesus, "Are you the only stranger in Jerusalem who does not know the things that have taken place there in these days?" (Luke 24:18). Certainly, to some degree every appointment generates some conversation; some even generate excitement. However, because of the perduring accuracy of the words of Rev. Dr. Martin Luther King Jr. that "11:00 on Sunday morning is the most segregated hour in our nation," there is often much conversation generated as a result of CR-CC appointments. Nevertheless, these conversations should be viewed as opportunities for evangelism and growth. Under few other circumstances would sustained dialogues and genuine relationships emerge.

I will soon enter the seventh year in my current CR-CC. My first six years of ministry were also in a CR-CC appointment. After twenty-seven years of ministry experience, I have been afforded innumerable opportunities to become more appreciative of the unplumbed potential of the church, specifically The United Methodist Church. I have served a variety of congregations, including urban, rural, suburban, multi-staff, small-staff, single-service, and multiple services. In my last appointment, I served as the senior pastor of St. Mark, the largest African American congregation in the Northern Illinois Annual Conference. (St. Mark is the second largest African American congregation in the North Central Jurisdiction.) Chicago has been identified over several years as one of the most racially segregated cities in the United States. The separation that we witness and experience is more than geographic, racial, economic, educational, and vocational; it is also spiritual. In spite of the increasing frequency of CR-CC appointments, our denomination is becoming less diverse. Many of our congregations are losing members and others are closing. The unmet need is increasing.

The role of the pastor is often conceptualized differently in CR-CC appointments. In many appointments, regardless of race or gender, the new pastor will need several months to be accepted as the leader of the congregation. In a CR-CC appointment, the new pastor is identified as being different *in addition to* being new. The ways in which the appointment is introduced to the leadership team (e.g., Staff Parish Relations Committee, Administrative Council) and congregation can unintentionally suggest that the racial and cultural differences will result in conflict. The pastor has to artfully navigate the nuances of the identity of being the new pastor and the one serving a CR-CC appointment. The differences between the new pastor and the congregation have to be minimized, at least initially, to allow the appointment to avoid becoming mired in any reservations related to the CR-CC nature of the appointment.

As the leadership team becomes more familiar and comfortable with the pastor's styles of leadership, administration, and preaching, the pastor and the leadership team should remain intent on fostering candid and respectful dialogue. The conversations should include one-on-one private conversations as well as small groups. The goals and expectations of the pastor, the leadership team, the superintendent, and the bishop should also be discussed regularly. These expectations may be modest and somewhat vague at the beginning of the appointment because of the uncertainty of the reaction of the congregation and the community to the CR-CC appointment.

The CR-CC appointment that I currently serve is thriving—our budget has increased over the past several years; we've ended the year with surpluses each year; families—both young and old, married and single—continue to join the church and participate in the ministries; the number of participants in mission trips continues to grow; the music and worship are powerful; the staff are not only talented but dedicated; and the total number of staff members has more than doubled. As with any congregation, we have our moments of tension and disagreement. However, we feel blessed by God for this phase of the journey and, like those who walked to Emmaus, we can say, "Were not our hearts burning within us while he was talking to us on the road, while he was opening the scriptures to us?" (Luke 24:32). Although there are many books that address leadership, management, and development that draw upon research findings from scientific disciplines, the art of carefully applying these principles and conceptualizing the nuances of CR-CC appointments needs to be explored further and appreciated more.

Christianity and Multiculturalism

Rev. William B. Meekins

Before I enter into the topic of Christianity and multiculturalism, I want to share a little information about myself and my background, to give perspective as we move deeper into the topic. I am the second oldest of eleven children, with nine of us living. My upbringing was not atypical, but there were a couple of things that helped to shape my reality from an early age.

My father, a United Methodist pastor, was always interested in exposing us to a lot of different things. In particular, he was concerned with shaping or constructing a worldview that was not limited by where we lived and who lived around us. He believed that one should "love the Lord your God with all your heart and with all your soul and with all your mind," and "love your neighbor as yourself" (Matt 22:36-40). We were taught that "neighbor" was beyond those living next door or even those who looked like us. Racial diversity was something that was valued, and it began to shape and develop my own worldview. As a teenager I was blessed to appreciate the uniqueness and the value of various cultures, as I had the opportunity to spend six weeks in Guadalajara, Mexico, and to spend one year in Spain as an exchange student. My parents wanted me to experience the world, because I struggled with my vision since birth, and they were unsure if my eyesight would hold out. I have been intentional about my education by seeking out predominantly white institutions and African American institutions of higher learning.

All of my life I have been Methodist or United Methodist. The founder of Methodism, John Wesley, was a Church of England priest born in Epworth, England, in 1703, and died in 1793. His vision was not to start a new denomination but rather he wanted the church to reach all kinds of folks. He was a pioneer and proponent of multiculturalism and is quoted as saying "the world is my parish."

There are four pillars that hold up Methodism. They became known as the quadrilateral. The pillars are scripture, tradition, experience, and reason. Scripture is primary, and the biblical narrative and Holy Scriptures are what shapes and molds Christians. Within the church there are traditions that have evolved over the years and provide meaning for the church. They help us interpret the scriptures and use our intellect to live into the life, meaning, and purpose that God has given to us. They also help us discern how we are to live in the world.

The scriptures are foundational in developing a biblical view for multiculturalism. For example, in the book of Ephesians is a call for us to find unity in the Spirit—working towards cooperative relationships and not forgetting that we are created in the image of God. Due to the fall we have allowed racial divisions and hatred, as lived out in apartheid, slavery, and in other ways that were/are discriminatory in nature. The challenge for us, as Christians who seek to be in community across the racial divide, is to use scripture and other methods, for example music, to begin the process of building relationships and community.

Thus, there is a foundation that leads one to believe that for the sake of the Christian church, we need to find ways to bring multiculturalism to the church and beyond. Before moving further, it is important to provide a working definition that can help us. The International Federation of Library Associations and Institutions, which is the global voice of the library and information profession, defines the term multiculturalism as "the co-existence of diverse cultures, where culture includes racial, religious, or cultural groups and is manifested in customary behaviors, cultural assumptions and values, patterns of thinking, and communicative styles." I define 'culture' as those values, traditions, customs, and language that may help to define a group of people, which is consistent with others definitions.

In 1996 I had the opportunity to visit China as an Ambassador through the General Board of Global Ministries. After visiting mission sites we shared stories about the ways mission dollars were being spent. We had arrived late at one rural village and as we were getting off of the van there stood three women singing "Amazing Grace" in Chinese. There was beautiful harmony as they sang with spirit. Despite the fact that we did not speak Chinese, we could connect with the song, because we recognized the tune. Words change but melodies do not. Music transcends cultures and languages. "Amazing Grace," written by John Newton in 1779, as cited by sources, is a popular and traditional hymn in the church. Traditional songs have a way of helping us to cross lines of division and separation.

John Wesley clearly desired a church for all cultures and people and was one of the early pioneers that opposed slavery, which was a tradition during colonization. This dehumanization was lived out differently once discrimination was no longer supported legally. Methodism's history in becoming a multicultural church has not been an easy pathway. Yet, since the merger to form The United Methodist Church in 1968, it has placed an emphasis on racial inclusion, with the hope of building multicultural congregations and affirming that we are one in Christ. This is not to say we are where we need to be.

The other two pillars that I have not given much attention to are reason and experience, with the exception of my brief commentary on my trip to China. My experience from traveling to five of the seven continents, and over thirty countries, has shown me that every culture has something to offer. I am often asked this difficult question: "What is your favorite country?" How can one answer? How does one say that climbing the Great Wall of China, or going inside any of the great pyramids of Giza in Egypt, or climbing the pyramids in Mexico built by the Aztecs, that any one of these experiences is better than the other? From experience it is reasonable for me to believe and see the value in connecting with folks from various cultures. It is not difficult to see that, from one family, God has created us, and has called us to love and live in peace and harmony as the body of Christ.

The Role of the Church to Support Inclusion of Different People

Rev. Dr. Albert Shuler

I was the first African American to be appointed to a cross-cultural/cross-racial church in the eastern North Carolina Conference of The United Methodist Church. There was no preparation for such a significant transition on the part of the cabinet, the church, with me. I felt I was dropped in the valley of dry bones to prophesy to bones in which we shared no commonality.

The next fifteen years were somewhat of a challenge, but I endured because of my faith in God. Throughout those years I learned some valuable and needed lessons, if we are to be a church and live in a multicultural world.

Nearly everyone in ministry these days is aware of the complex tapestry of cultures that forms the backdrop of how we operate as church in the twenty-first century. A multicultural setting is not something new in The UMC. That has been the story of the American church for over two hundred years.

I would like to address an area that is frequently overlooked: Just what do we really want? What are we trying to achieve? Can we set goals for this kind of ministry, even progressive goals that lead us into an even more effective ministry in multicultural settings?

I would like to focus on what is often the implicit goal of ministry in our churches and move onto a set of progressive goals that can help shape or direct us in our ministry, churches, boards and agencies, schools, and so forth, as well as provide the beginning for truly living out the Gospel that calls for our "Oneness" in Christ.

The goals are:

Reducing Conflict
Recognition of Others
Respect for Cultural Differences
Healthy Interaction between Cultures

Reducing Conflict

It is important for most people engaging in ministry in these settings to reduce conflict. The conflict can be on two levels. It may be, and often is, between two or more groups who experience tension in their relationship with one another. The tension may show itself in resolutely avoiding one another, competition for space and other resources, or outright conflict. The pastor views this as a setting in which conflict has to be mediated so that people involved can get along or, even better, fit in.

Conflict between groups is real and very hard to reduce. Sometimes it need to be addressed immediately with clear measures, especially if the conflict becomes violent, either verbally or physically. But such conflict cannot be treated merely as a problem to be solved. Ultimately relationships have to be formed, and building relationships takes time, patience, and a vision of where we hope to end up.

But there is another level of conflict—conflict within pastors themselves. Most feel uncomfortable and confused about what to do. They would rather the problems go away or hope some outside solution will present itself. Pastors, too, belong to various cultures. Many people are not totally aware of their cultures until they are confronted with cultural differences.

It is more difficult to analyze one's own culture than the culture of someone else. But without understanding one's own culture as one culture among many—however powerful and dominant that culture may or may not be—one has little chance of interacting successfully with others. One of the reasons why this is important is that one needs to feel secure in one's own cultural identity in order to deal effectively and healthily with other cultures. It helps people to realize that cultural difference is not a simple deviation from their norm but a manifestation of a more complex interaction.

Recognition of Others

How do we enter into that complex interaction? It begins by recognition of others. In most multicultural settings, the first reaction is to try to avoid or ignore differences. This takes two forms. It sometimes takes the form of ignoring the presence of another group by rendering them invisible. The other reaction is to cover over differences with rhetoric of "we are all brothers and sisters in Christ".

It is of course true that we are all brothers and sisters in Christ, and we are meant to live in unity and harmony. But the use of rhetoric is frequently a way of ignoring the realities and the tensions that intellectual interaction often brings. The only way to unity is through acknowledging the church's catholicity—the many tribes and tongues, peoples and nations that constitute the church. This is important because, despite efforts to ignore cultural differences, it is the differences to which we are continually drawn in interaction. Difference in accents, clothing, and social patterns are too salient to be ignored. Sometimes that difference leads to stereotyping and prejudice, making generalizations about others. Sometimes it leads to outright hostility.

Respect for Cultural Differences

If recognition of the other is the beginning of the journey toward intercultural relationship, respect for cultural differences is a description of that journey under way. Tolerance may mean putting up quietly with difference, perhaps with the silent hope that eventually it will go away. Respect, however, means coming to the point that one values the difference in its own right, which adds to the richness of our relationships and to the richness of the world. It means coming to see the cultural difference of the other not as a deviation from some norm, or a failure to reach a certain level, but rather as having intrinsic value.

Healthy Interaction between Cultures

The word healthy is important here, since much of the interactions between cultures is often very unhealthy. It may be marked, on one hand, by stereotyping, prejudice, unwarranted suspicion, racism, and even overt verbal and physical violence. On the other hand, it may be characterized by a stifling romanticism that glorifies difference as a last ideal of one's culture or a childlike stage, which will eventually move up to one's cultural level.

Healthy interaction is based first upon confidence about the value of one's own culture and a sense of security that is not threatened by the encountering of difference. Second, healthy interaction means that two cultural groups interact so well that they can point to each other's shortcomings. This is a very advanced stage of healthy interaction.

Summary

These four goals represent development of intercultural relationship, from an initial acknowledgment of other groups and a beginning commitment to journey along together to sustain healthy interaction. What are the implications? There will be *obstacles of intercultural communication* that a group might present, such as language. Therefore, it will be necessary to *provide communication training* and *build relationships*. We need bold biblical vision to challenge us to serve a rich and varied church.

Conclusion

The thesis of this book is that leading cross-racial and cross-cultural churches has great relevance for both the current and the changing context of The United Methodist Church. The purpose was to provide practical tips to church leaders and clergy who are leading cross-racial and cross-cultural churches, not just inform them of theories.

First, we have attempted to show that to build and create healthy, fruitful, and growing United Methodist Churches, pastors and leaders in cross-racial and cross-cultural appointments need to know and understand key concepts and trends. Second, we urge both pastors and lay leaders of cross-racial and cross-cultural churches to apply the insights to their ministry settings. As we discussed in the introduction, to build and create healthy, fruitful, and growing congregations, pastors and church leaders need to understand the changing context of their ministry and to respond effectively. We also emphasized the urgent need of evangelism and a younger generation in ministry and mission of cross-racial and cross-cultural churches. We hope that, while written from a United Methodist perspective, this book helps all congregations respond to the changing context of ministry.

Recommendations for Further Reflection

1. Develop and Discuss Case Studies

Develop and discuss case studies of the local church and community that you are serving. As you develop your case studies, keep in mind three critical questions: Where is God in this event or situation? What is the biblical reference for this case study? What actions should we take to transform individuals and the world? Churches as a community of faith should relate communal identity to the surrounding culture and should communicate to the wider world.

2. Create Your Own Beloved Community

How can you be a faith community in your church and your community? We suggest first that you read the following Bible passages and reflect on them as an individual and as a group: Isaiah 43:18-21; Luke 4:18-19; Acts 2:43-47; Ephesians 2:8-9.

3. Practice Spiritual Disciplines

What is a spiritual discipline? According to our Wesleyan tradition, spiritual discipline has two dimensions: works of piety, or personal holiness; and works of mercy, or social holiness.

Works of piety include reading, meditating on, and studying the Scriptures; prayer; fasting; regularly attending worship; healthy living; sharing our faith with others; regularly sharing in the sacraments; Christian conferencing (accountability to one another); and Bible study.

Works of mercy include doing good works, visiting the sick, visiting those in prison, feeding the hungry, giving generously to the needs of others, seeking justice, ending oppression and discrimination (for instance, Wesley challenged Methodists to end slavery), and addressing the needs of the poor.

Making disciples, growing vital congregations, and transforming the world is part of a spiritual adventure that is empowered and guided by the Holy Spirit as churches engage in the means of grace.

Spiritual goals are accomplished by connecting the means of grace with proven vital church practices, such as planning, strategic direction, prioritization, clear focus, and alignment.

4. Create a Worship Service for Your Congregation That Is Intentionally Cross-Cultural

We suggest and recommend that pastors, church leaders, and worship committees, with input from church members, create a Sunday worship service that is biblically grounded, theologically sound, and culturally relevant in the Wesleyan tradition.